MAKING A
COMEBACK

MAKING A COMEBACK

A WOMAN'S
GUIDE TO
RETURNING TO
WORK AFTER
A BREAK

MARGARET
KORVING

BUSINESS BOOKS LIMITED

Copyright © Margaret Korving 1991

The right of Margaret Korving to be identified
as the author of this work has been
asserted by her in accordance with the
Copyright, Designs and Patents Act, 1988

First published in Great Britain by
Hutchinson Business Books Limited
An imprint of Random Century Limited
20 Vauxhall Bridge Road, London SW1V 2SA

Random Century Australia (Pty) Limited
20 Alfred Street, Milsons Point, Sydney
New South Wales 2061, Australia

Random Century New Zealand Limited
9–11 Rothwell Avenue, Albany
Private Bag, North Shore Mail Centre
Glenfield, Auckland 10, New Zealand

Random Century South Africa (Pty) Limited
PO Box 337, Bergvlei 2012, South Africa

British Library Cataloguing in Publication Data

Korving, Margaret
  Making a comeback: a guide for women returners,
  and their employers.
  1. Great Britain. Job hunting
  I. Title
  650.1′4′0941

ISBN 0-09-174651-5
ISBN 0-09-174415–6 pbk

Typeset in Sabon by 🇦 Tek Art Ltd, Croydon, Surrey
Printed and bound in Great Britain by Mackays of Chatham PLC

CONTENTS

FOREWORD

So you are thinking of returning to work? Perhaps you are in your twenties or thirties, with children nearing school age, and are considering a part-time job. Or you may be in your thirties or forties, wondering what retraining could do for you. Whatever your age, is it really true that some employers go out of their way to recruit older people? Yes, it is – in some jobs, maturity is an asset!

Perhaps you have found just the right child care and long to respond to your former employer's offer of your old job back – if only you weren't so concerned about learning to cope with today's new methods. When you left, people were using manual filing systems and typewriters – now it's computers and word-processors.

Margaret Korving knows all about these problems. Though her youngest son is now in his teens, she vividly remembers rushing round the shops in her lunch hour and worrying about finishing work in time to meet her son from school. She, too, has had to learn to use a computer and word-processor followed by many an evening hunting for lost sports kit! So her book is as much about *how* to combine work and home as to *which* jobs to choose and *where* to train for them.

As Equal Opportunities Director of Midlands Bank plc, I am glad to recommend this realistic and practical guide to any woman who is thinking of returning to work. Whether you are just browsing through the vacancy pages, thinking about a refresher course or training for something new, I urge you to put aside the past and challenge the world of work. Enlightened employers will value your maturity, develop your skills and make you a very welcome 'returner'.

Anne Watts
Equal Opportunities Director
Group Personnel
Midland Bank plc

INTRODUCTION

A NEW DEAL FOR LATE STARTERS

For 25 years I have worked as a careers writer. The questions I have answered by post, in print and through radio phone-ins must number many thousands. Yet, there were always two problems to which I felt I had no satisfactory answers.

The first was: 'Where can I find work that fits in with the needs of my home and family?' The second was: 'What careers can I train for now that I am 40?' Though I always did my best to make positive suggestions, I was aware that opportunities were few and far between. I never dreamed that the day would come when employers would actively seek people in such situations.

Today, with an ever-decreasing pool of school-leavers to train, employers nationwide are competing to attract women returners. Boots the chemist and Thistle Hotels offer term-time contracts. Midland Bank are introducing workplace nurseries. The Civil Service has removed or greatly extended upper age limits for most jobs. Part-time Registered Nurse training, during school hours and with school holidays off, is available at several hospitals.

For women who want to be self-employed, the Government provides a £40-a-week Enterprise Allowance to help them through their first year. For women who want to be managers, the Open Business School provides distance-learning all the way to an MBA. For women who want graduate careers, Access courses provide entry to degrees in subjects as diverse as speech therapy and law.

This book is about making the most of these opportunities.

CHAPTER 1

WHERE ARE YOU NOW?

If you are aged between 25 and 50 (55 for many occupations; 60 for a few), there has probably never been a better time for you to look for work or training. Not since World War II, when workplace nurseries and after-school playgroups were provided everywhere so that women could replace men in the factories and fields, has there been such an upsurge in demand for women workers.

All the same, in the last ten years, women have seen so many changes in the employment world, that it's understandable if they find their new popularity hard to believe. What about all those closed coal-mines and steelworks which threw so many men out of work? And the takeovers and mergers which left experienced senior managers surplus to requirements – sometimes 'redundant' for years?

Many women now being urged to return to work have seen their teenage son or daughter hunt hopelessly for any kind of job, or even a chance to get some 'work experience'. Though things are better now, if you are one of the women whose family has suffered through a lack of jobs, you will need some convincing that returning to work is not going to take the chance of employment away from your partner or your children.

It may seem unlikely after all the years of worry about finding employment for school-leavers – but this country is running out of teenagers. In 1987, a Government survey discovered that between 1987 and 1997, the number of people aged 15–24 will fall by 22 per cent. This includes *all* young people in that age band, from unqualified school-leavers to graduates and young professionals.

Already, this shortage of young people (which results from a fall in the birthrate in the 1960s and 1970s) has affected education. Many local papers now report arguments about which secondary schools should be closed or merged because there are not enough teenagers to fill them. A few years ago, you may remember that many primary schoolteachers couldn't find work.

Now, it's the third level of education which is being affected. Further education colleges, polytechnics and universities are having to make a real effort to attract more mature students, because they know they won't fill their classrooms with school-leavers. And employers, who not so long ago were cancelling apprenticeships and training schemes because there were far too many unemployed teenagers to absorb, are now not only restarting these forms of training, but raising the upper age limits for entry to them, in the hope of getting some new adult recruits.

Yet, however hard employers and colleges try to attract young entrants to training schemes and job vacancies, there will still be a need to make up that missing 22 per cent of young people. This is where you, the woman returner, come in.

Again, the figures tell the story. The number of adults (both men and women), in certain age groups, will increase between 1987 and 1997. The 'missing' teenagers will have to be made up by attracting people from these older age groups into work and training. For example, the number of people in the 23–34 age group is expected to rise by 11 per cent by 1997. And though only a slight increase is expected in the 35–44 age group, the number of people aged 45–55 is expected to increase by 25 per cent – more than the missing 22 per cent of young people.

Naturally, as these figures refer to both men and women, many of the 'available' workers will already have jobs. The pool of newcomers on which employers and training authorities hope to draw is mostly made up of women who have been at home for some time – perhaps to raise a family, or to look after an elderly relative, or because they simply didn't like the job they did before becoming home-makers, and didn't need to go back to it to earn money. These – and you are probably among them – are the people the country needs to tempt back to work.

ARE YOU AVAILABLE?

Some of you may be longing to get back to work – for money, or company, or just for the sheer satisfaction of doing a job you always enjoyed. You may not know of any local opportunities; you may want to do research into child-care facilities; or you may want to discuss the whole matter carefully with your partner (and your children, if they are old enough).

Some of you may want to return to work, but not to the same kind of work you once did. We're often being told that people should expect to change their careers two or three times in a lifetime, but in the past, finding a second career for which you are eligible to train has not always been easy. One of the good things about being a woman returner today is that employers and colleges need you so badly that they are tossing aside former rigid age limits, and widely relaxing entry requirements to allow as many as possible likely trainees to prepare for second careers.

You might like the idea of returning to work, but on a 'toe in the water' basis. Perhaps, you reason to yourself, your toddler really won't miss you if you do a couple of night shifts at a hospital or on a switchboard. He or she will be in bed with Daddy on hand all night, and you'll return in time to get the breakfast. Or you may like to try out several jobs as an office 'temp', working hours to suit you. (This is a particularly good idea if you are asking yourself whether you'd like to train as a social worker or a hotel manager or in a department store, or something else. Employment agencies can often arrange for you to work in several different environments, giving you an inside view of possible careers, and allowing you to talk to people already in them about their snags and advantages. No-one will blame you for moving on at intervals: that's what 'temping' is all about.)

HOURS TO SUIT

This is the title of a lively book by Anna Alston and Ruth Miller about flexible work patterns being tried by various employers. Some take any hours you can offer. My local paper recently carried an advertisement from a hospital seeking domestic help from anyone with time to spare, from a single evening to a full week. A luxurious restaurant wanted waiting staff at lunchtimes, evenings or weekends. On the 'education' page was news of an Access course (a preparatory course for people aiming at degrees or diplomas or professional qualification courses) held during school hours only, for which no qualifications were required. *These opportunities are multiplying by the week.*

YOUR OWN BOSS

Some of the services previously offered by big firms are now being offered by small companies and self-employed individuals. These might very well be run by two or three women working together or, depending on the amount of work involved, by a single woman working from home. For instance, two or three women could run a maternity fashions service, designing and making clothes and selling them on a party-plan basis. Or an individual teacher of English as a foreign language could take students at home or visit their homes. There are dozens of opportunities of this kind. (You'll find some ideas in Chapter 9.)

Many colleges now offer short business courses, some just a day long, allowing participants to investigate ideas before taking the plunge. If a whole day is out of the question, maybe you could quite easily arrange to attend, say, ten evening classes on a once-a-week basis, with a neighbour looking after your elderly father, or a friend baby-sitting for you. If you're interested in self-employment and you think your home commitments make you best suited to work from home, it's worth checking out all the Government help you can get, which could include a £40-a-week Enterprise Allowance for 52 weeks, to get your business off the ground. (See Chapter 9.)

MAKING TIME TO WORK

You may feel that, although you would like to work, you already have plenty to occupy you (even if you don't like all of the tasks involved), and can't find time to do a job. Investigating part-time, sessional and occasional work opportunities may help. What could help even more is to sit down and list everything you do in a week, from taking and collecting children to and from school to washing and ironing.

If you are going to take a job, some of the everyday tasks you now do will probably have to be done in a different way – perhaps a way you've never considered before, because (a) it wasn't necessary and (b) you may have felt it was uneconomic. For instance, washing – and in many families – drying clothes is something a lot of home-based women do in their own washing machines. If you go to work, you'll probably find that it's more practical to use a launderette for a 'service wash' once a week, or perhaps once every two weeks, doing small amounts of washing and drying in your usual way. You may never have needed to 'cook ahead' and fill your freezer, so that people can help themselves to meals as they wish. Time saved on washing and drying clothes could be used to do this – saving even more time for your job.

Another bonus of making maximum use of new technology to run your home is that the knowledge gets passed on to your children. A recent letter from my student daughter mentioned that in her first fortnight at college, she was asked by several students if they could go to the launderette with her, because they'd never had to look after their own clothes at home.

I'm not suggesting that, as a working woman, you must have every known gadget (I was in my fifties before I afforded the microwave, and I still use the instruction book when I'm doing anything new with it!), simply that a few wise investments can help to release large amounts of your time for the things you really want to do. They can also be very cost-effective: going to work will probably enable you to afford household gadgets you never considered before. In any case, most people go to work for something over and above the pay. If you really want to return to work, and if the only way you are going to manage it is by investing gradually in household time-savers, you will probably feel that it's worth it. Women accustomed to budgeting for a whole family are unlikely to put deposits on every gadget they've ever needed within the first week of their new job.

Freezers save on shopping time and, at the very least, mean you've always got something in stock for an emergency meal. Very busy people with high earnings may fill their freezers with ready-made meals that only need heating; those with hungry teenagers and no time will probably make sure that the freezer always contains sliced bread, beefburgers, sausages and oven chips. You can learn what's right for your family as you go along. People who love to cook, and who perhaps have an elderly relative to cater for, may enjoy making up a set of individual cottage pies or fish pies, which can be used in one-portion sizes when needed.

Another time-saver is a microwave oven. Find out if there are any local demonstrations or evening classes on 'making the most of the micro'. You can, of course, teach yourself, though expert tips can be indispensable. For example, it saves a great deal of time to cook chops or chicken pieces by microwave, and then brown off the result in a conventional oven. This isn't a cookery book, so I won't give more examples, but the bonus of the microwave is that it cooks in minutes rather than hours.

As well as examining *how* you do your work, try re-organizing the time spent on chores. There's no law that says men should mow lawns on Sundays, working women should shop during late-night sessions on Fridays, or the best meal of the week should be at the weekend.

Make a list of chores and responsibilities (with when they happen, and who does what), take a good look at it and consider whether, even before you start work or college, there may be new methods worth trying out. You've nothing to lose by at least talking over possible changes.

If you're a single parent, solely responsible for a child, it is even more vital to make a list and establish your priorities. Of course you'll need to investigate child-care arrangements, but don't forget your responsibility to yourself, too. At what time in each day are you going to have a nourishing, quiet meal? You need at least a little time and space for yourself. How are you going to fit in time to play with the baby or listen to what the school-age child has been doing all day? You're not Wonder-woman, so you'll need to plan.

If it all sounds very stressful, remember that you are likely to feel much more capable and relaxed by having a change from being at home and by meeting other people, rather than being always in charge, as you may be at home with a child. It's usually worth giving any new scheme a try: remember, you can always stop going to work if it doesn't work out. But you might be pleasantly surprised at how working outside the home, even for a few hours, can boost your morale and confidence.

SELF-EMPLOYMENT
While looking at your circumstances, skills and needs, consider whether it might be better for you to work at home than for an employer. The independence and flexible hours sometimes offered (though not always guaranteed) by self-employment are attractive to many women returners.

If you think that working at home is a real possibility for you, look very carefully at your list of chores to see how you might reorganize the work to give you a clear daytime working space, when people can ring you up and find you in; when you can sit at a job and concentrate on it; when you have someone around to take over your home and/or family responsibilities. (Self-employment is dealt with in more detail in Chapter 9.)

MAKING A FRESH START

Another big advantage of the great teenager shortage – and thus the urgent need to recruit adult women to fill the gap – is that all kinds of courses and job training schemes formerly barred to the over-21s are flinging open their gates to take in mature students. Many nursing schools now welcome students up to 45 or 50, sometimes 55. The country's first BA (Hons) in Public Relations considers mature students aged from 21–60. And there's a very happy trainee police officer in the West Midlands Police who has just been accepted at age 45, after being told eight years ago that he was 'too old'.

There are now many examples of employers who have positive attitudes towards training and promoting older people, and of colleges where it's your willingness and ability to learn that matter, not your age and, in many cases, not your qualifications. Having worked out where you are in your life, and what time you have available for work or study, you must now decide on the kind of return to work that is right for you.

MEMO TO EMPLOYERS

Before they can even consider a job or training opportunity, returners need to know what hours and/or shifts and/or days are on offer to them. Whether you use job centres, employment agencies, displays on your own premises or advertisements in newspapers or on radio, *always* specify the hours of work. If you can also specify any age preferences – and may be add 'people outside these limits will be considered' – you will increase your chances of getting a satisfactory range of applicants. Headlines like, 'Evenings to Spare? – Earn With Us', 'School Holidays Off?' or 'Vacancies – Full & Part-Time – Most Age Groups', are reassuring because they instantly convey the message that you've thought about the home responsibilities of possible job applicants.

CHAPTER 2

WHERE DO YOU WANT TO BE?

Once you have decided that you do want to take up work of some kind, it's time to think about your job priorities. After reading the first chapter, you should have worked out how much time you can spare, to work, train or study. What are you going to do with the time you've made available?

'Earn some money!' may be the answer for many people. There can't be many of us who couldn't lead a better life with some extra money. It's an important point to consider when you are discussing your return-to-work plans with your partner, or children, or perhaps with the person you're paying to mind an elderly relative while you go out to work or take a college course.

Many women whose husbands support them still long for money *they* have earned, to spend as *they* please. There will always be people who tell you that you have the wrong priorities; that they would spend their time and money differently. But each of us has the right to set our own target. Earning extra money is a perfectly respectable reason for going back to work.

However, earning money takes effort, and you must be sure that you can cope with the effort you have to put in. It may be very tempting to respond to an advertisement that offers £120 for four night shifts at the supermarket, but have you ever stayed up all night and tried to sleep during the day? (Have a rehearsal; you'll need to organize your other commitments and get people's co-operation when you are working, so a trial run won't hurt and could highlight any potential problem areas.)

The same sort of preparation is very wise if you are returning to a job that was well within your capabilities five or ten years ago. Jobs change – often for the better. As I sit writing this book at my word-processor, which lets me correct any errors as I go along, simply by typing over the mistake, I think back to the time when I'd have had to use liquid paper to cover up mis-typing, and then back again, to the days when typewriter erasers took the surface off the paper as well as the ink.

Whatever the job, you can be almost certain that it will have been altered considerably by the technological changes of the last decade. Take advantage of any updating the employer may offer, or any refresher courses at local colleges (see Chapter 6).

To set yourself a target, think through what you feel you should be achieving, with approximate timings. For instance, in your first week back at work after a long break, you can reasonably aim at getting to know two or three of the people with whom you'll be working, and finding out how much of the work you're doing is the same as it was before, and which parts of it have changed since you were last in your job.

By the end of your first month, you should be able to identify what you may need to brush up on, and how best to do it. You may have a helpful supervisor or Personnel Officer who takes an interest in returners and suggests training. Ultimately though, the way you update will depend on both your responsibilities at home and your long-term ambitions. It can be better to cope well with a fairly routine job for a while and build up a reputation for reliability, while at the same time keeping things going at home. (Some feminists may think this isn't fair, but it is more important to be realistic.)

For some kinds of work, different methods may have to be learned, like feeding information into a computer and getting answers from it instead of using ledgers or files. Don't be frightened by such processes: it can be a lot easier to type in a name and reference number, and then press a key that gives you information about the person than it once was to check a card index, locate a file and search through quantities of past correspondence for what you needed.

READ ALL ABOUT IT
With some careers, you can catch up more quickly getting back issues of magazines or journals that relate to your field of knowledge and finding examples of new methods or special

achievements. In fields like science and nursing, teaching and catering, there are plenty of journals to read. If you've belonged to a professional association, they'll help too. (See Chapter 6.)

You might find that you need – or want – to update your qualifications. Individual trade and professional bodies, or national organizations, like the Business and Technician Education Council, the Royal Society of Arts and the City & Guilds of London Institute, can always advise on your next step, and often direct you to a particular course in your locality.

Within six months, you should begin to feel quite confident working at the level you achieved before your 'time out'. You might gain confidence well before this time. Indeed, if you find you slip back into work as if you've never been away, you may decide to set a different target – perhaps promotion, a job move or higher qualifications.

The entertainer Ben Lyon (older readers will remember him from radio shows during World War II) used to say, 'Activity breeds activity', ie, the more you do, the more you'll want to do. Don't be surprised if your targets move as you go along. Circumstances will play a part, too. Your children may become more independent, then you can work longer hours. You might be offered a promotion that involves job-sharing: doing more responsible work for half the working week, with a colleague who also wants to combine home and work.

LOOKING AHEAD

The possibility of turning a convenient job into a fascinating career is something that may seem light years away when you are at the stage of managing three mornings a week in a routine job while your toddler is at playgroup. This particular time can be heavy going for the returner who may wonder if it's all going to be worthwhile. You need to remind yourself that any change in life (getting a job, moving house, joining a social club) deserves a fair trial. I've told the following story before in newspaper articles, but it deserves repetition because it shows how one tentative move into work can lead to great things.

The returner in question didn't really want to return to work at all even though she needed the money. She had two small children at primary school and a very sick husband who was expected to be in hospital for many months. She told employment agencies she could only consider jobs within school hours and with school holidays off. What turned up was a job as a part-time nursing assistant at a local hospital for the mentally handicapped – something she had no knowledge of, and which she found very saddening when she was first taken round the hospital.

As the weeks went by, she learned ways of communicating without speech with patients who had never learned to talk. She proved so good at this that the hospital authorities wanted to send her on a speech therapy course – but that, of course, was impossible with her home responsibilities.

Instead, she found a way to study for a well-known drama school's qualification in speech and drama, attending evening classes while a friend looked after the children. It helped her hospital work and she later took a few private pupils at home – children who wanted to prepare for oral exams.

Eventually, she moved to the local further education college where she taught spoken and written English to teenagers on Youth Training Schemes and helped with the drama club. She continued working for the hospital on a voluntary basis and, as her teaching responsibilities grew, took examinations to become an examiner of speech and drama students.

She now combines college work with home teaching and examining at drama festivals and competitions. Incidentally, her husband became well and strong again during this time and her children did well at school. If asked, she'd probably deny that she'd set herself any particular targets, other than to do what she was doing more effectively; but simply taking each opportunity as it came along moved her up the career ladder.

CHANGING DIRECTION

Many readers of this book will have grown up during the years when the expected careers for girls were teaching, nursing and secretarial work. Nothing wrong with that – if you happened to be a born teacher, liked caring for people or had the temperament and ability to keep perfect order in an office when all around you chaos raged.

Nevertheless, in my long and enjoyable years as a careers adviser, I have discovered that a substantial number of women see their return to work as a chance to do something quite different from the career they once had – even to escape from it. (An organization called 'The Escape Committee' is very effective in helping teachers who want to escape from the classroom to make a job change.)

For all kinds of reasons, women may have taken a job recommended for them by their parents, their school or the careers service. Many succeeded perfectly well, despite disliking the work or the environment. On the other hand, having now been alerted by the media to equal opportunities and fresh starts, many women want to follow up what was once only a distant dream and retrain for a satisfying career.

DIFFERENT ROUTES

There are now many more opportunities for mature people to train in careers that were formerly the province of young people. When I once wrote in a magazine to a woman of 28 who wanted to try for drama school that she should have a go, I was greatly surprised to get a letter, a few days after publication, from another woman, aged 40, who had had the same dream, taken and passed the audition for drama school and was training as an actress. 'It's hard – but it's my heart's desire,' she said.

In later chapters of this book, I focus on actual examples of training courses and methods of qualifying for different careers. You could well find that your one-time dream job is among the examples I cover here, or in the books I suggest for background reading (see page 127.)

However, there may be some targets that are still inaccessible. As I write, the upper age limit for entry to most medical schools is 30, and you need pretty impressive qualifications, too. I say 'most' medical schools, because every organization breaks its own rules when appropriate. If, for instance, someone who was part-way through the medical course in youth, and had to break off because of some family tragedy, re-applied at 32, with a suitable job background and enough money to manage on, she might be taken on.

Veterinary science is another door likely to be closed against late starters, however keen. Veterinary schools are wildly over-subscribed and have to turn away teenagers with A-level grades like AAB. The only difference the shortage of teenagers is likely to make here is that the schools may have to take people with slightly lower A-levels.

These are two examples of targets you may never be able to reach, however hard you try. In such cases, it's worth considering whether there are other targets you could reach which give you some of the job satisfaction you'd hoped for from your first choice. There are useful books to help you choose another target. Typical are: *A Doctor – or Else?* by John Thurman and *What Can a Teacher do Except Teach?* by Barbara Onslow. Librarians and careers officers can be very helpful in suggesting books and leaflets that could prompt alternative ideas for you.

At the same time, you need to think for yourself about jobs that are closely related to your first choice, or skills that might bring you into the work environment you see as ideal. Read all you can about them. Talk to people doing them. You'd be surprised, for example, how nursing has changed in the last ten years: the most recent story I picked up from the national press related to a hospital specializing in heart surgery where an operating-theatre Sister was being taught to dissect out a blood vessel for use in a transplant operation. The system was so new they didn't really have a name for the job – 'cardiac technician' was one that came to mind, though as there are already cardiology technicians (who take heart readings), it didn't really describe what the Sister did.

The interesting aspect of this example is that the surgeons had decided that nurses would be more satisfactory assistants than junior doctors in taking responsibility for this type of surgery. They argued that by the time junior doctors became really skilled and swift at this job, they had to move on to a different part of their training, leaving the heart surgeons to start training yet another novice doctor. It seemed much wiser to make it a specialized job for a trained nurse, who would stay with the job and provide a reliable, continuous service.

Nursing, of course, has changed in many other ways. Most of us know and value a 'practice nurse' to whom you can go not only to have a dressing changed or an injection given, but with any question that you hesitate to bother the doctor about. For many women who as school-leavers wanted to be doctors because of the opportunity to take independent responsibility, nursing is worth very careful investigation.

Like the reader who wrote to me, you may want to be an actress. It may be quite impossible for you to go to drama school, but you could get into a theatrical environment by learning to be a costume or scenery designer, wardrobe mistress, stage manager. One woman I know used her secretarial skills to get a job in broadcasting. Her subsequent promotions involved becoming responsible for all the administrative work of an arts festival. She is now set on becoming an arts administrator (which can involve running a theatre, promoting an opera group or managing a ballet company) and is combining study with part-time amateur dramatic work to build up her skills. This is satisfying work, among people who share her interests, and is strongly related to her long-ago dream of having 'something to do with the theatre'.

The would-be vet who becomes a publicity officer for an animal charity or paints wildlife greetings cards; the teacher who finds satisfaction in training as a nurse for the mentally handicapped, patiently instructing them in independence skills; the girl who wanted to be a window dresser in a fashion shop, and who, as a grown-up, moves from shelf-filling in a supermarket to stock control in a furniture and fabrics store and then (having had some stock and distribution experience) to trainee display worker in a department store – all these people are finding their own routes to their own targets.

If you have a dream job, it is vital to work out all the ways you might reach it, or get near to it, so that you won't forever be looking over your shoulder and saying, 'I might have done X if I had only tried.' And, if you have to take a less-than-satisfying job for a few months, or even a few years, don't tell yourself to forget all about your original ideal job. Employers, colleges and professional institutes are constantly finding new ways to train people, and accepting different kinds of entry qualifications. If you keep in touch with what they are doing, you will be the first to hear about the latest part-time course, distance-learning route or extended upper age limit for employment.

REACH FOR THE SKY

If you were ambitious before you took a career break, it's highly unlikely that you will be content simply to pick up where you left off and forget all about career development – thank goodness! Although being single-minded has its virtues, it would be an odd kind of world if top jobs went only to those people who thought of nothing but work; who had never known what it was to cope with a change of circumstances, or to overcome a difficulty in their path.

For many responsible managerial and professional jobs, it can be of immense value to have had what the social work profession calls 'life experience'. Social work is, not surprisingly, among the professions which actually *prefer* mature entrants, the theory being that having coped with domestic responsibilities and/or worries and/or problems of one kind or another makes the would-be social worker more able to comprehend the difficulties, and the strengths, of others.

Maturity is valuable in many different kinds of work. If you are in a job where you supervise young people, you can look back on your own teens (perhaps at your own teenagers) and adopt an approach to which they will respond.

Dare I say it – having coped with home responsibilities and made one's share of mistakes makes the returner a more responsive manager? A couple of years ago I changed my accountant, or rather the accountant was changed for me by the practice as a new female member of staff joined them. Self-employed people are often frustrated at the thought of coping with accounts; there seem to be far more urgent things to do, like the work your clients are waiting for and the sales drive you have to make in order to have more work to do when the current commission is over. My female accountant (who I discovered was a part-time ACCA returner) clearly recognizes this and gives gentle advance warning when figures are needed.

During a bad patch, when I was working and coping with illness in the family, she took over all my bills, receipts and notes on scraps of paper and turned them into coherent accounts. Of course, she expected to be paid for this, and perhaps a young male accountant would have been just as thoughtful in the same way. But I can't help thinking that her own experience of juggling job and home may have made her more understanding of other people's problems.

One of the questions that often crops up when a professional person is returning to work after a break is how well they will work under a young head of department. An answer that will help you get the job is: 'I shall probably find it helpful in many ways. I expect someone using the latest methods will be able to help me update. I have a student son/daughter, so I'm used to young people at home.' If, when you get your job, the young boss seems hard to satisfy, hang on to your patience and make sure he or she realizes that you are aiming to work well, rather than compete. This doesn't stop you getting promoted in the long run if you are worth it, whereas if you worry a young boss in your early weeks as a returner, he or she does have the power to limit the range of work you get to do.

If, when you return to work, you slip back into the atmosphere as if you had never been away, you'll almost certainly want to develop a career plan for going onwards and upwards. To do this, you need to study (a) your present employment and the scope it offers, (b) the actual job you do, and what demand there is for people with your skills and qualifications and (c) how your occupation is regarded in the general labour market. For instance, you might find that your knowledge of food products would be better used in a job as a catering trade representative than as a delicatessen manager. If it's difficult to get back into publishing, you might be able to adapt your writing skills to public relations work, or your knowledge of contracts to working with a literary agent. Jump into the employment pool wherever you can find a space, then dog-paddle while you have a look around. You could well find that the jobs you were too young to take at 22 are waiting to be discovered by you at 40. Rein back your ambition while you decide on the best direction to take – then go for it!

OAKS AND ACORNS

Do remember that just as jobs outside the home rarely stay exactly the same year after year, so home-based work can flourish or die away. Most of us know women whose knitting is so fast and flawless that it's a pleasure to pay them a reasonable sum for making jumpers and jackets. A few knitters, though, are so original and successful that they find themselves, without much effort on their part, suddenly running knitwear businesses, from home, by mail, through market stalls or for local boutiques.

The same can apply to many other areas of expertise. Jennie Hawthorne found 30 Ways to Make Money in Writing, and wrote a book with the same title. I've had many letters from women who became Registered Child Minders, partly for a little extra money and partly, often, to provide company for their own toddler, and who subsequently found they wanted to run playgroups, manage nurseries or train as infant teachers.

Unfortunately, I've also heard from women who invested in expensive secretarial equipment, then found they couldn't get enough work to cover their costs; so you need to control your 'paying hobby', 'home business' or whatever you call it, carefully.

If you want to confine your return to work to a small portion of your free time at home, you may have to be tough with people who urge you to expand and make lots of money. As time goes on, you yourself may want to build a business, but if you feel that all you want at the moment is to set up a modest spare-time enterprise, don't let yourself be badgered into dynamism. Working is something you do to please yourself as well as to earn money, help others, gain status, etc.

While working on magazine programmes at the BBC, I was given the chance to prove myself as an investigative journalist. I was sent out, tape-recorder in hand, to interview a man described as an exploiter of poor old pensioners who were paid peanuts for knitting babies' bonnets and mittens which the wicked exploiter subsequently sold on his market stall for a substantial profit. When faced with this accusation, the wicked exploiter gave me a list of the names and addresses of the pensioners he exploited. 'Go on and ask them what they think,' he said. 'None of them need to work for me. I think you'll find we're doing each other a favour.'

This proved to be absolutely right. The knitting pensioners – and I obediently interviewed a good number of them – all said the same thing; roughly, it went: 'I know Mr Jones makes a good profit on this knitting I do for him. I don't care at all. I love knitting, and if Mr Jones didn't supply the free wool and needles, I couldn't afford to do it at all. Considering that he also pays me for my hobby, I'm very well satisfied.' As a piece of investigative journalism, this was very disappointing for my producer at the BBC, but it taught me that there are reasons other than money, status, companionship, etc which people take into account when work comes their way.

What matters is that *you* know your reasons for wanting to work, and that you set your own targets – adjusting them as you go along, and as your circumstances change. When you were 16, you might have had to do as you were told. Now you are 26, 36 or 46, you can decide for yourself. And once you know where you are going, you will make a positive impression at interviews and when you restart work or begin a training course. That makes life easier for everyone, including the employer.

MEMO TO EMPLOYERS

Women returning to work after a break need to be reassured that they will be taught new skills and allowed time to get into the routine of working again. 'Flexitime' can be a big attraction, but you need to explain that it's not just a question of being able to adjust starting and finishing times. Mothers will be particularly glad to know they can 'save up' hours to take off when a child needs to be taken to the dentist, for example. As confidence grows, opportunities to gain higher pay or promotion by passing skills tests or studying for qualifications will be appreciated. Employers should study their trade or professional journals to find out about new ways of training, intensive courses, updating on their premises or distance learning facilities. Put up any details of courses you run alongside the usual notices about 'Vacancies', 'Welfare', 'Meetings', etc. Giving the name of someone who can be consulted about courses or training makes people much more likely to follow up the offer: it's hard to walk into an office full of unknown people and say you want to find out about training.

CHAPTER 3

WHAT DO YOU HAVE
TO OFFER?

There are four main questions to answer when assessing what you have to offer an employer:

1. What do you *know* you can do?
2. What can you *prove* you can do?
3. What are your *personal* abilities and advantages?
4. What can you *learn* to do?

By taking time to go through the four questions and answering them thoroughly, you will usually find you have a far wider range of career possibilities than you may have realized. And, though you may not be able to follow up a special ambition immediately, knowing that you have the potential to do it will make you more content with the work you get in the meantime, and encourage you to plan how you will develop your career.

One of the things we all learn as we go through life is not to 'show off'. If it hasn't been drummed into you at home by parents, brothers and sisters, it surely will have been at school, where, even if you had ten O-levels or were Captain of Games, you learned that it was tactful to keep a low profile. We can all feel friendly towards the person who is hesitant about discussing her achievements, but may feel threatened (depending on how tactfully it's done) by the person who rattles on about her recent successes.

When looking for a job or a place on a training course, it is important to strike the right balance between modesty and pride. For instance, if you're one of those remarkable people who has managed to obtain an Open University degree by studying at home, you should be sure that people not only recognize your graduate status, but realize the extra effort you have had to make in order to get your degree. At an interview, you might say something like, 'Of course, I would have loved to go off to university, but it wasn't possible with two children to look after, so I chose the Open University course instead. Even so, there were a few moments when the family grumbled about having to watch OU programmes at breakfast!' Any personnel officer should get the message that doing a degree at home is far from being an easy option and that they are not just being offered someone capable of studying and reasoning at a high level, but someone who can do this despite a backdrop of children's questions and the ping of the microwave!

The question anyone with the responsibility of choosing an applicant must answer (whether it's a job or a place on a course under consideration) is, 'Can this person cope with the work?' or 'Will this person keep doing the work?' or sometimes, 'Is this person capable of doing more demanding work?' If you were choosing someone to take care of your children or run your home, you would want some evidence that the person you choose was reliable and suited to the responsibilities involved. So, too, will the people who are considering you.

WHAT CAN YOU PROVE YOU CAN DO?
This is where you take pen and paper and look back at your life, noting down every exam you have passed (not just at work: remember your St John's Ambulance Brigade training or successes in Public Speaking competitions), and the different kinds of activity involved in each job you've done. **NB:** This is not a curriculum vitae but your private file from which you will later take facts to create your CV.

Once you are past 21, no-one cares much about your primary education, though for jobs that involve education it might just be worth writing down 'Scholarship to X girls school at 11/13'. Older personnel officers will know what the competition was like many years ago to get a scholarship to the school named, and people considering candidates for jobs in an academic setting may well be interested in information they regard as related to educational matters, even if the achievement isn't strictly relevant to, say, running a Teachers' Resource Centre, or working as a school secretary.

At the age of 15 or 16 though, the major national examinations make their appearance. Among the qualifications you can prove may be passes in the GCEs or SCEs, or, if you're older, the School Certificate/Matriculation exam. (Older readers may find it helpful to know that today's personnel officers may not be aware that those who did very well in School Certificate could obtain London Matriculation, which made them eligible to apply for a London University place.) You don't want to waffle on about these kinds of qualification, but it may help, for public service and local authority jobs (and certainly if you are applying for a college place) to add a few words on the subject. You might write: 'School Certificate (date), including English, Maths, Science, Foreign Languages. Achieved London University Matriculation, with option of university place.' You can expand on the details at interview, but it never hurts to alert the interest of the VIP reading your history at the earliest possible stage.

Personnel managers and college admissions tutors are likely to be most familiar with the GCE (or SCE in Scotland), and for some jobs or courses, the grades you achieved could tip the scale in your favour. List all subjects you passed, with grades. If you have studied a subject up to exam level but didn't pass the exam, mention your background knowledge of the subject in your application letter. College application forms often ask you to include the subjects you have failed as well as those you have passed. (It's not just idle curiosity; it could be helpful to have studied a subject up to exam level, even if you didn't pass. You have some sort of background knowledge on which new skills could be built.)

When filling in job application forms, it may be quite unnecessary to list all the subjects in detail, taken straight from your personal history. Many advertisements simply ask for someone with 'Five O-levels, including English and Maths at grade C or better'. You might simply respond with 'Seven O-levels, including English (C) and Maths (B)' and then expand on the subjects at the interview.

To return to the personal history file which you are creating, take exactly the same approach when listing other exams from which you'll later create a CV. Expand on the subject studied if it helps you remember a useful achievement. You may perhaps have taken an exam subject that involved a project – make a note of that project. The fact that for your Modern History exam, you interviewed a group of 80-year-olds about their lives, using a tape recorder, could be worth mentioning on a job application for a market research interviewing assignment; or for social work training; or for work in a shop selling what the trade call 'brown goods' (TVs, videos, radios, tape recorders, etc). It could also interest admissions tutors for paramedical and nursing courses, where the ability to communicate well with elderly people could be most valuable.

Our teenage years are when many of us first become involved in leisure activities outside school. Your son or daughter will probably have a much wider range of spare-time activities than you did, but *you* may nevertheless have produced plays for the local drama group (demonstrates organizing and management ability), passed Red Cross or St John's Ambulance exams (shows interest in caring for people and taking responsibility in an emergency) or experienced working holidays abroad (developing independence as well as gaining experience of other lifestyles and languages). Be careful not to miss out anything which might enhance an interviewer's impression of you.

SKILLS AND QUALIFICATIONS
Happy are those whose previous career required them to follow a mapped-out path, attending day-release or block-release classes or studying by correspondence for related exams. Anyone who has closely followed developments for 'Credit Accumulation and Transfer' in the academic world will know how valuable this may be – even many years later. Colleges nationwide are now establishing a system of evaluating qualifications of national or professional bodies in terms of making the holder eligible to take degree or other advanced courses, even though he or she may lack A-levels.

Qualifications and awards being evaluated in this way include BTEC National and Higher awards, the old BEC and TEC awards that BTEC replaced and examinations of individual professional groups, such as the Communication, Advertising & Marketing Certificate or the examinations of the Chartered Institute of Management Accountants. An annual handbook is published by ECCTIS (Educational Counselling and Credit Transfer Information Service), giving details of all these opportunities.

Qualifications obtained and exams studied for are not the only valuable components in this context. For many courses, 'appropriate work experience' is also credited as a way of satisfying entrance requirements. So if, like many people, you did the sort of job that didn't necessarily involve passing exams in order to get more responsibility, write down what you actually did. Again, remember that you'll be drawing on this detailed information later, in order to create a CV. 'Secretarial work' doesn't really convey the fact that you were responsible for arranging conferences, booking halls, finding hotel rooms for visitors, hiring projectors, liaising with caterers, and so on. 'Managing a shop' may not convey to the reader that you were in charge of window display, supervising two juniors, seeing representatives, chasing up orders, keeping stock records and handling all financial affairs. Write down what you really did; you may want to draw on it later to demonstrate that your past experience includes work similar to that on offer.

This chapter is concerned with the value of being able to *prove* what you did, so gather together any written evidence of your work responsibilities. In times past, employers used to issue testimonials or written references. Perhaps you kept yours? It's a little olde-worlde to send photocopies of them with job applications nowadays, but a lot does depend on the job applied for. You might not want to send them off to the jazzy boutique in the High Street, but they could be appropriate for a job with a security firm or any work that involves confidentiality – for instance, in a legal firm or an accountancy practice.

When compiling your personal history, list your jobs in order, starting with the most recent one and working backwards to your first job. Name the firm, giving the title of the job you did, eg, 'Secretary to directors', Teacher (slow learners) with special responsibility for music', 'Travel agency clerk', and then describe your main duties. Add the name (or job title if you can't remember the name) of the person who can be approached for a reference. You can select extracts from this detailed job history later, as required for a CV or course application form.

WHAT DO YOU KNOW YOU CAN DO?
You must now think about what you've learned *during* your career break. Many women who never managed to pass GCE Maths have found their way through the maze of family

finances, coping with mortgage, credit cards, hire purchase, foreign exchange on holiday, and so on, as well as being able to measure up a room accurately for wallpapering and adapt the instructions of a knitting pattern to fit someone of a non-standard shape. If it has been your responsibility to manage the finances, or you've had to teach yourself basic home mainten-ance, make a note of it. Otherwise you might forget to mention it when you are applying for that fascinating job in the interior design agency.

Life and its problems has a way of giving us all experiences that challenge us to discover exactly what we can do. When I was a schoolgirl, I loved to read hospital romances and occasionally wondered if I might make a nurse. Indeed, when I started to write for a living, I also took a part-time job in the local hospital to help make ends meet. I was pleased when the Matron suggested I should train as a nurse, but felt then that I was still too squeamish.

A few years later, one of my children developed an illness that at intervals required the parent on the spot to give instant emergency treatment which could include injections and oxygen to aid breathing. Such emergencies generally woke us in the middle of the night, when though half asleep and frightened to death, there was no opportunity to be squeamish or feel faint. Now when I visit hospitals, that old schoolgirl longing to nurse often surfaces again. This time I know that the careers books were right – if you really want to nurse badly enough, you'll learn to cope with feeling scared and squeamish.

Perhaps you, too, have had an experience of this kind that lets you put 'home nursing' among the list of things you know you can do. I tell my story to illustrate how we all take for granted the skills we have to develop as time goes by, often forgetting they could be relevant to a job. Whether you've cared for a sick child or an elderly parent, or perhaps become the sort of neighbour to whom everyone comes with their troubles, it could be a job indicator – nurse, social worker, police officer, ambulance driver, dental assistant or school secretary.

Many women are surprised to discover just how good they are at caring for children once they have some of their own. Nursery nursing or teaching may have been the last careers you thought of when you were a school-leaver, yet here you are with children, and sometimes not just your own but everyone elses'.

Write down any involvement you've had with the younger generation, including helping at playgroups, being on a parent-teacher committee, listening to children read at an infant school, and so on. It is a valuable potential job skill. You might train to teach, or to be a youth leader, housemother or warden in a student hostel. It's a useful gift, too, if you want to run a hotel: families will return year after year to people who can help their children enjoy the holiday.

You probably wash, iron, cook and mend without giving these skills a second thought. Do you do any of them really well? A couple of sisters in the town where I live had a highly successful business for many years making stage costumes and ballet tutus for local dancing schools. My 84-year-old mother has a stream of relatives and friends patiently waiting for one of her individually designed Mexican-style tapestry cushions. No, she doesn't sell them, but if she was younger and wanted to, the gift shops would be queuing up. Write down any skills you have developed in the domestic arts that might well be valuable in a paid job or for a home business.

Some people, given problems, don't react by seeking out an expert opinion or finding their own way out of the difficulty – they get angry and start a campaign. We have these people to thank for all the charities which raise funds for people and animals in need, protect historic buildings and places of scenic beauty, and even make public officials write forms in plain English. Are you one of these campaigning people? If you've initiated, or take a responsible role in, a national or local society or campaigning group, put this down under the heading of 'What do you know you can do?' You may later want to draw on it in answering a job advertisement that asks for 'ability to work on own initiative' or 'experience of administrative work'.

WHAT CAN YOU LEARN TO DO?
Government schemes keep changing, not only in their names (TOPS, WEEP, YOPS, YTS) but in what they offer. At the time of writing, three vital government schemes are: ET – Employment Training; Career Development Loans – which allow you to borrow money to pay your training fees for the course you want (including private courses); and Enterprise Training – courses to prepare you for self-employment. (They are described in greater detail in Chapter 5.)

The Employment Training scheme normally combines training at work with studying at college or a training centre for recognized qualifications. That this is worth having is something few people would deny. Employers often complain that people have no 'work experience', so if you can get on a training course that combines work experience with study for qualifications, you're getting a good deal.

But in case your main reason for returning to work is to earn some badly-needed money, I think I should mention that the official ET scheme pays you only the benefit you would be entitled to if you were not training, plus approximately £10 a week (plus extras in some cases – see Chapter 5). This may make it a hard decision for someone who would like the planned, supervised training and the chance to get qualifications offered by ET, but who has debts or other commitments that call for the most money that can be earned in the shortest time.

Remember, though, that working lives are getting longer. This week, a giant new hypermarket was advertising for staff in my local paper. Their age limits: 16–75! So don't be depressed if your home commitments mean you have to stay with a high-pay, low prospects job for the time being. After all, you may find that having the high pay means you can afford to take a home-study course for better qualifications once you've settled into work and established a routine at home.

Another source of training and qualifications that you may have hesitated to consider in the past is your local further education college. There are now only a few who really don't want to know about mature students and this attitude is unlikely to last once such places realize that they will have to start closing down classes if they don't attract mature students in place of missing teenagers.

Happily, though, the vast majority of further education colleges are welcoming and helpful to mature students. Many of them have sent me enthusiastic letters and encouraging leaflets about their courses. So if you happen to be passing your local further education college, why not pluck up the courage to walk through the doors and see what's on offer. Most colleges have an entrance hall where they display leaflets about their courses. Often enough, too, the receptionist on duty will be a mature person (possibly a returner like you) and you'll feel you can ask if there's a course in the particular subject you want.

If not, ask for a college prospectus.

The worst thing that could happen is that you could ask on a day when the receptionist's cat hasn't come in all night or a group of students has been rude or one of the lecturers won't believe her new textbook has not arrived and been mislaid. On such a day, you might get, 'No we don't have a prospectus. The leaflets are over there ... [or] ... you have to write in ... [or] ... which department do you want?' In which case you shrug your shoulders and decide to ask in the library instead.

Nine times out of ten, though, the receptionist will fall over herself (or it might be a him, getting office experience on a business studies course) and try to help, proffering daytime and evening class lists, telling you about Saturday classes or when exactly people enrol. Don't be surprised if people assume you are enquiring on behalf of your son or daughter – FE colleges are still mainly the province of the young. But if you say you're looking for information about courses for mature students, people will usually be very helpful.

This isn't idle encouragement. On the occasions when I've failed to get any reaction by writing to a college, I've often telephoned the general switchboard and asked if there's anyone to answer questions about retraining courses or courses for mature people. The response has always been heartwarmingly friendly.

The skills you can most readily learn at evening classes often involve using equipment, such as cookery, typing and wordprocessing, dressmaking, upholstery, and so on. It may be useful for you to note that in most counties, colleges have got together and decided that because equipment is expensive, one college will take responsibility for hotel and catering teaching, another college for printing courses, another for building trades, and so on. You might be re-directed to a college in the next town for this reason, so don't think they are just trying to get rid of you.

If you are thinking of taking a course with a particular job in mind, it could be helpful to get the views of your local Jobcentre (or any private employment agency, like Blue Arrow) on the value of the qualification or skill you're hoping to gain. You don't necessarily have to take their advice, but their approval would be reassuring.

WHAT ARE YOUR PERSONAL ABILITIES AND ADVANTAGES?

Once upon a time, not so long ago, when employers automatically seemed to reject anyone not thin and aged between 25 and 35, I used to advise older job-seekers to add a passport-size photo of themselves to their CVs. It catches the eye immediately, and if the reaction – as it often is – is for the employer to say, 'Gosh, this woman says she's 51. You'd never believe it', you are in with a chance.

It doesn't work for everyone. It certainly wouldn't work for me – fat and bespectacled, I have a lot of sympathy with the dear old Wizard of Oz who was much more impressive behind his curtain of green smoke. But if one of your personal advantages is a pleasant face and figure, use it. Others would love to have the opportunity.

Some people like the telephone and find it particularly easy to talk to someone they can't see. If you are such a person and know that you do yourself credit on the telephone, then ring round for jobs or information about courses. Don't forget to get people's names. It is important for everyone's sake to know that you were talking to Mary Bryce or Lindsay Pine or Joshua Fox (these are three real people who possess a delightful telephone manner, so here's a chance to acknowledge it). Apart from the fact that you may need to get in touch with them again, you may want to mention their names in connection with a written application, ie, 'Having talked to your secretary, Julia Adams, today, I understand that you would like details of my voluntary work experience . . .'

If you are better on paper than in person, by all means build on that ability. Take care, though, to keep a copy of what you write, and be prepared for someone to ring up and ask you about anything you've mentioned in a letter or listed on a CV. Go over it again before you attend an interview because your interviewer will have used your letters or application form and CV in deciding what questions to ask. (More about preparing for interviews in Chapter 4.)

Are you mobile? Lots of us take it for granted that we have a driving licence and can take our turn at the school run. But if you have a driving licence and the use of a car, the range of jobs, and the hours you can work, stretch out considerably. Many of the occupations in what's usually called the 'service' sector, ie, hotels, hospitals, sales, social work, etc, involve irregular hours. Employers (as well as women themselves) are often less than happy at the thought of women going home on late night buses. Having your own transport is definitely a plus factor on an application form. It may also mean you have access to a college course that you couldn't reach by bus or train.

Do you have a job partner? I'm not talking about a helpful husband or male companion here, but the possibility that you have a friend who wants to job-share with you. Though increasingly, and particularly in the public sector, employers advertise job-share opportunities, it's often necessary for two sharers to make direct application to employers. For instance, if the pair of you keep seeing the same job advertised in the paper week after week, that employer is likely to be susceptible to a well-worked-out job-share plan. While keeping your own priorities in mind, take into account the fact that you need to present the aspects of yourselves that will most appeal to the employer. Look for special advantages: for example, 'We can both type but Jenny also has word-processing experience', or 'We can arrange to work two and a half days a week each, but if either of us is off sick, the other will stand in for her and make up the time'.

MEMO TO EMPLOYERS

When considering returners who have had a substantial work gap, look carefully at the content of the jobs they did before the gap. They may well only need updating in modern methods. Consider how they have been occupied during the gap years. Any participation in community affairs – being a school governor, membership of a tenants' association, recording for a local Talking Newspaper – should encourage you, as it shows their interests have not been limited to the home. Highlight any exam passed, no matter when: it shows the candidate can reach a specific target and demonstrates staying power. If the qualification is unfamiliar, check its meaning in *British Qualifications* (Kogan Page), or ask a Jobcentre adviser or careers officer to identify its value. Listen to the voice behind the face of a job applicant, and look for the personality behind both. Your clients are less likely to be worried by grey hair than by a grumpy temperament!

CHAPTER 4

CONFIDENCE TRICKS

We have Robert Burns to thank for that confidence-sapping verse that goes: 'O wad some Pow'r the giftie gie us / to see oursels as others see us!' Though it's probably good for us to be reminded that we all have failings, most people are far more likely to sell themselves short than boast about their achievements. Indeed, in case you're one of the people who feels she has little to offer, let me offer you a quote from an Admissions Tutor on an extended Certificate of Qualification in Social Work course at Stevenage College:

> 'Students come on the course saying, "I've only been a Mum for ten years" . . . "I've only been a foster Mum" . . . "I've only been looking after my handicapped child". We find they come with a lot of talent and a lot of life experience, which is more important than A-levels. In the first year of the course, they catch up with the students with A-levels. . .'

Similar comments are made by training officers in industry, university and polytechnic tutors and the organizers of 'New Opportunities for Women' courses (see Chapter 5). Stepping off the work ladder to spend time at home gives you a different kind of life experience, not necessarily less valuable than that gained by the person whose time is wholly devoted to advancing in a job.

Some valuable qualities will have to have been developed by anyone with a home to run and others to care for, such as adaptability, planning skills and good timekeeping. Unlike the women in the TV ads, most of us rarely have the time to compare washing powders, soak away our cares in a deep refreshing bath or worry over-much about the sex appeal implied by our choice of coffee. We are more concerned with seeing that the washing is discovered wherever it may have been dumped by the children, that all the hot water has not been used by the time we want a bath and that there is coffee of some sort available. Women at home are expected to be able to do a lot of different things well and on time – abilities that will be gratefully recognized when they return to earning.

In addition to planning ahead and keeping to a timetable, when at home, women are expected to be able to continue with the usual routine during any kind of emergency, from a child sent home from school with fever and earache to the impending arrival of a business colleague who needs to be fed, watered and entertained. ('Whatever happened to the table mats? Oh no, there are only three decent wineglasses left'.) Anyone who has coped with this sort of lifestyle is unlikely to fly into a panic when the photocopier jams or a careless customer drops a jar of pickled onions in the main aisle.

But, as a famous newspaper once said of its competition, 'You've got to be in it to win it'. Until you are actually there in the workplace, demonstrating your flair for coping despite provocation, interruption and time pressures, you can't begin to use the extra life experience you've gained at home. It's making yourself enter the competition that so many women find daunting, so I will now try to cover some of the main worries and how you might consider defeating them.

LOOKING THE PART

I've yet to come across the women's magazine that doesn't run jolly articles about dressing for work, often entailing the expenditure of sums like £150 for a neat little suit or recommending a cheerful red outfit rather than dull old grey (thus ensuring that you'll be known as the Woman In Red from day one in your new job). Prospective returners are often among those selected to be 'made over' by magazine fashion and beauty experts, and who would deny that it's encouraging to see how much more attractive anyone can look after being titivated by an expert?

However, in attempting to be helpful, it's possible to make the 'appearances' aspect of returning to work seem far more important than it is. Only in nineteenth century novels are women at home identified by their aprons and slippers, and it is highly probable that your wardrobe already contains clothes perfectly adequate for work outside the home.

Obviously the sort of work you want to do will affect your choice of clothes. If you're planning to get a job as a receptionist in a beauty or hair salon, then your clothes and grooming need to be top-notch. If you're planning to teach in an infant school, frocks that will come up smiling after the paint has been washed off are clear winners. Many jobs involve wearing a uniform and in this case, pretty underwear that you won't be ashamed to be seen in at the hospital or store changing room could be a lot more important than what you wear on the journey to work.

If you feel rather dated by your clothes or know your range of outfits is limited, and you can't start investing in new things until you've earned some cash, don't look at the magazines for ideas, tempting though they are. Go out and look at the women you see leaving work. Town-dwellers will have no difficulty finding role models in the rush hour. Countrywomen may need to drive or take a bus to the nearest town to get an overview of what today's women at work are wearing. Don't be surprised if 90 per cent of them dress just like you: few jobs demand top fashion and even TV newsreaders dress simply to face the cameras and their millions of viewers.

Being tidy is important: personnel officers may find it hard to believe in your organized mind if you are constantly pushing a lock of hair out of your eyes (remember the criticism faced by Shirley Williams) or have to rifle through your handbag for a tissue. And as 'down at heel' has moved into the English language as meaning someone who appears a shabby failure, treat yourself to a session at the heel bar – be extravagant and have all your shoes done at once. It's a comparatively small expense that adds considerably to a sense of security, like having a three-pack of tights in the bottom of the wardrobe.

Interview clothes are usually different from work clothes, but the difference needs to be subtle. You want to show that you've made an effort to look well-dressed for the occasion. At the same time, you must avoid looking as if you've put all your best clothes on and are too immaculate/frivolous for the job. Avoid anything new and untried, like shoes that could cripple you as you're given a tour of Head Office, or any outfit that only just fits, and that could result in you worrying about whether your skirt is riding up instead of the questions being asked.

For most job interviews, the sort of outfit you'd wear to visit your mother-in-law, or to a parent-teacher evening at school or even a hospital visit to a friend is probably most appropriate. The image you are aiming at is that of a pleasant, unfussy, organized person. You might get it by buying that £150 suit I mentioned and wearing it to church a few times so that it doesn't look brand new, but if you don't have £150 handy, you probably have something just as adequate in the wardrobe already.

If you are given the chance to see where you'll be working, take it. It will show you what the other workers look like (and also point out any hidden snags, like a smoker at the next desk if you're inclined to be wheezy). You might be able to create the opportunity to see the workplace for yourself at the end of the interview. Interviewers usually ask, 'Is there anything you would like to ask?' If it has been a friendly conversation and you feel fairly sure you're in with a chance of the job, it would be reasonable to say, 'Is it possible to see the workroom/Purchasing Department/diet kitchen?' If you get the job, having had an advance view of your new workplace will make you feel less like a cat in a strange garret.

SPEAKING UP FOR YOURSELF

I think most of us have heard the joke about the wife and mother who went to endless trouble to plan and serve a sophisticated meal when her husband's boss came to dinner, only to find herself leaning over to cut up the boss's meat into bite-size portions as she regularly did for the children. Whether or not it ever happened in real life is anyone's guess, but if you've spent the last five years persuading children to eat their carrots and tie their shoelaces, you could be a bit out of touch with adult conversation.

Again, beware of expecting this to be a giant problem. Presumably, as well as reading *Topsy and Tim* or *Charlie and the Chocolate Factory*, you listen to the radio and watch TV. You may even get your hands on magazines and library books, though newspapers can be difficult if you've got young children around.

There remains a trap for the woman returner that can block

her progress up the career ladder. Men, it seems, manage to separate their home/work lives, and when at work talk about impersonal things like sales targets, the local one-way traffic system or the best type of exhaust system to fit to a car. Women drift into personal anecdotes (what happened when Tim first saw the rabbit) or discuss whether it's safe to keep feeding the children on microwaved meals each evening. For this useful sidelight, which I recognized as true the moment I read it, I have to thank Kathryn Stetchert, whose book *The Credibility Gap* will be valuable reading for women who sense that their career prospects are being slowed by an inability to manage interpersonal relationships at work. She says: 'Men like to talk about things and activity; females prefer to talk about people and feelings.'

If this rings a bell with you, and if you think your lack of recent experience of anything to talk about other than 'people and feelings' will be a handicap, there are things you can do to widen your interests. For a start, rearrange your work at home so you can watch some daytime TV discussions – the sort where many people voice different opinions: you can always do the ironing while you watch. Or listen to radio programmes that once again involve a range of people expressing their views on topics of the day. Radio 4's *Any Questions* and *Any Answers* provides instant updates on what's worrying the world. Local radio stations often have the same kinds of programme with lots of phone-in input from listeners. (Who knows, you may well be prompted to join in yourself – another step forward.)

Take advantage of any chance you may have to talk to people who are not relatives or neighbours. By all means attend the parents' evening at school. I am told that teachers often dread these events quite as much as parents do, and tremble inwardly when they face you over their lists of pupils' names.

In addition, see if you can squeeze out a little time in which to attend an evening class, or maybe one or two 'one off' Saturday classes in a subject that interests you, at your local college. If you feel really out of touch with other adults, don't distress yourself by picking a subject like speaking in public. It's more constructive to have a happy day learning flower arranging and coincidentally giving yourself the chance to make a couple of new contacts with whom to share a coffee break.

Don't be cast down if you don't find anyone particularly

friendly at the first class you attend. The others could be as shy as you are, or they might be little groups who've come because they share flower arranging at the church, or met at some other evening class and want to keep in contact. Though you are more likely to make contact with people who share your interests at a class or club devoted to the subject, it's not guaranteed. You may find a best friend waiting to be met in the cloakroom of your child's dancing school, or reading the job vacancy cards at the Jobcentre. Deciding to look out for other adults who'd like to be friendly is the really important factor.

WORKING TO A TIMETABLE

We all do this all the time; the timetable we use is our own sense of priorities. Yet, if you are to return to work, you must make a space in which to be out of the house (or occupied with your business, if you go for self-employment). As I said in Chapter 1, it's possible, by listing everything you do during the week, to re-arrange your responsibilities to allow a useful time in which to work or retrain.

There is no one ideal way of organizing your time to combine work and home responsibilities. I once read the biography of a young widow who did all her housework at night. This was her worst, loneliest time, so she occupied it by washing and ironing, peeling the next day's vegetables and baking cakes and scones for her young family. She didn't sleep very well, so going to bed in the small hours, thoroughly tired, meant that the sleep she did get was deep and restful. Heaven forbid that you should have to use your time in this way for the same sort of reason, but it's one way of looking at how you can adjust your life to your circumstances and the time available.

I'm a morning person, and given the okay (husbands have to be considered as well as bosses' requirements), I'll put my alarm on for 5 a.m. and get in three good hours of writing before I have to down tools and start cooking breakfast. Not every lifestyle would lend itself to this sort of arrangement, but if you look at your own, you may find that you can not only find time to work or study, but also let your family benefit from your action. 'Give a little – take a little' works for most people. While your daughter's at the Brownies, you can concentrate on your videoed Open University programme. When you go to your evening class, your family can enjoy their favourite ready meal from M & S. If you have Mary-next-door's daughter to tea and to do her homework while she's at her office job, Mary-next-door will take your toddler between breakfast and playgroup when you're doing an early shift at the hospital.

When talking to voluntary work agencies, the one factor they keep emphasizing is that they don't mind how little time a volunteer offers as long as it is regular and reliable. 'We'd much prefer someone who can come in from 10 a.m. to 12 noon once a week than someone who says she can come three afternoons a week and often doesn't' was the way one spokeswoman put it. This is something to bear in mind when you are looking at jobs or courses. Plan a timetable which you can keep to. Interviewers can be very persuasive: 'We would understand, of course, if your child was unwell and you were unable to come one morning.' It's flattering to be needed, particularly after a long break, and your confidence gets an enormous boost when you're asked if you can work every day. But try to get into the habit of saying, 'May I let you know tomorrow?', and going home to consider what's realistic. It is better to regretfully reject a job offer and wait for something appropriate to turn up than take on too much and find that you're the one who has to be regretfully rejected at a later date because you can't manage the hours.

FACING UP TO AUTHORITY

It is natural and normal to be a bit apprehensive before an interview, and, when you get the job or the place on a course, to be a bit hesitant in the first few days, even weeks. Have you done the right thing? Will the family suffer? Should you have waited until the children were at secondary school/university/married/in Australia?

Being uncertain about making the right decision is one thing. Fearing the person who may ask you to make it is quite another, and yet most people when asked would say they are apprehensive at the thought of an interview (or going into a crowded room or speaking in public). It's probably a throwback to memories of first days at new schools, when not only the people in charge but also your equals were all an unknown quantity.

Here's my tip for facing up to interviewers. Take a good look at them and try to see what they might be like outside the interview room. Are they much younger than you? Then they may not be long out of college and themselves anxious about making the right decision, knowing their own jobs are on the line if they choose the wrong person for the job. Are they your own age? Then they, too, probably worry about their mortgage, their children and what to have for supper. Are they much older than you? Then they may well wish they were in your shoes, with a long span of years ahead of them, and they'll certainly remember what it was like to worry about money or family or being lonely.

I can't claim credit for that approach as it was shared with me by a radio producer many years ago when I confessed I was feeling very scared at the prospect of interviewing an MP and a trade union leader, known to be at each other's throats politically and with strong views to express. 'They're just people,' said my wise adviser. 'They've had the same trouble in getting a taxi to the studio and worrying that they'll be late. They're probably worried that they won't be as good as each other and that their supporters will be disappointed. They're almost certainly more nervous than you are.'

How often, when we are dealing with apparently awkward people, are we unaware that their budgie might have died (that their cat is at the vet, their son failed his GCSEs or that they are awaiting the results of a medical test). We're all human, and we mostly share the same sorts of experience, which means that every person who is an interviewer has once been an interviewee. To the familiar advice that you should take a deep breath and wait to be invited to sit down when you go in for your interview, I'd add, 'Remember, the person you're going to meet probably has a life much like yours'. Or, even shorter, 'Remember, his budgie might have died'. I promise you it works wonders with interview nerves.

PRACTICE POLISHES
Only in ballet or opera, and probably only then if you are Margot Fonteyn or Pavarotti, can one say that 'practice makes perfect'. On the other hand, practice does polish. The first time I gave a coffee morning for the neighbours I got into such a flat spin about hoovering the bedrooms and getting in a really nice choice of biscuits, I had to borrow a jar of coffee from my neighbour. It's the same with most other activities. The more you talk with other adults, the more confident you will get. The

more you expose yourself to new situations and challenges, the more able to cope you will be.

Perhaps it isn't easy for you to get out and meet people, but could you get people to call in and visit you? Novels dismiss the chat over the garden fence, but it has its values for someone who spends much of her time alone. In the same way, you might find it hard to face up to asking for advice at the Jobcentre, but you could make a start by asking the librarian on the enquiry desk at your public library if he or she could reserve a particular book you want. You might visit a hospital patient who would otherwise have no visitor. You could help make costumes for the school pantomime. It may sound very low profile to the confident lady who is bursting to get back to her career, but don't knock it; some of the women you supervise may have had to overcome just such confidence problems. If you are a professional person, get back in touch with your own kind by joining the nearest branch of your occupational society or institute (headquarters addresses in *British Qualifications* or the *Directory of British Associations*, both kept in libraries). You will almost certainly be welcomed to local meetings and national seminars and there may be refresher courses or returners' meetings (see Chapter 6).

If you have teenage children, they may be a great help in boosting your confidence when you are considering returning to work. Before you dismiss this suggestion – you may be coping with an impossible 15-year-old who worries you to death by staying out till midnight – it's worth bearing in mind that between 14 and 18, most of the world is concerned with telling you what to do: it's a nice change to be asked for your opinion, whether it's on a change of hairstyle, how the buses run into town between 7.30 and 8.15 a.m. or whether they think it's better to take a morning job without much future, or go on a college training course for three months. Be tactful: you want to leave yourself an escape route in case your highly original daughter suggests you have an auburn tint or 'sign on' and take a home-study course. You might say, 'I'm collecting opinions from people who know how we live about my next move. What do you feel is best, x, y or z?' That way no-one's feelings are hurt if in the end you follow your own nose and take the job you first thought about. Meanwhile, you will have discovered how those around you feel about your decision.

The final confidence trick I have to offer is that you are a grown-up now. You don't have to stay in that job or continue with that course if you discover it's all wrong for you. It's not a question of Woman Returner versus Rest Of The World. You are quite entitled to change your job, take another break, decide you would like to do something different or find that instead of studying for a degree, you'd like to learn practical skills on the job. Making a fresh start does not have to mean a permanent change in your lifestyle. If you've made a wrong choice, well, you're probably canny enough to put up with it for a while, doing the best you can to satisfy, while you look around for something that might suit you better. But you've managed without working before (the advantage of coping during the 'gap' years), you could manage again, if necessary.

So, while you do your best to please, nothing is irreversible unless, that is, you take the decision not to try at all. Now that is difficult – because it's not the things we try to do we regret, but the things we wished we'd tried. Bear this in mind when you're debating whether or not to complete that application form.

MEMO TO EMPLOYERS

You are almost certain to meet many returners who have been away from work for a substantial period, but whose application forms show they are quite capable of doing the work you have to offer. Help them to feel at ease during an interview by beginning with questions about things that are familiar to them: their journey if you can see they had a bus or car ride to the office, their children (don't make this sound as if you expect them to rush home every time one has a tummyache), why they've decided to return to work. Give them a 'breather' by telling them about the job that's on offer, or about your company and its benefits. Then you might draw attention to anything in their past history that suggests they may be suited to the work.

If you feel that you are talking to someone whose commitments make work for you a real impossibility at present, say, gently, that you are a bit doubtful whether they could manage the hours or training required, but that you'd like them to consider re-applying when their children are older or they are able to work more hours. It's no kindness to leave people in desperate hope when there is really no justification for it. It can also be valuable to give a leaflet about the firm and its working conditions, pay, hours and welfare arrangements to anyone you hope to employ. It is often hard to remember everything that is said to you at an interview and written material reinforces important facts.

Where you can, be positive about the scope for returners in your company. A British Telecom Personnel Manager once endeared herself to me by saying that as she was a mature graduate who had been given a chance by BT, she always looked out for other mature graduates when attending university 'Milk Rounds'. 'I know what stamina is called for to take a degree later in life,' she told me, 'and it's valuable at work. Also, mature people are less likely to move on, to the benefit of someone else, after you've trained them for two years.'

CHAPTER 5

FINDING OPPORTUNITIES

WHAT'S IN A NAME?

If, as you are reading about new opportunities for women, you think, 'Well, they haven't got anything like that where I live', you could be in for a surprise. Providers of training – local and national – are often very restrained in the way they promote it. Often enough, if you happen to miss the particular issue of your local paper in which a course for returners is advertised, you won't get a second chance to learn about it. Most colleges work to a very tight budget and may not be able to afford more than one advertisement.

Even the writers of books which list courses can have difficulty persuading colleges to part with information about their attitude to mature students or provision for returners. Without naming names, there are a few universities and polytechnics, and still more colleges of further education, which never respond to requests for information. You can only imagine letters going astray once or twice. After that, I suspect that someone at the college concerned is saying, 'Why should we tell her/them about our courses. We can easily fill them from one advertisement in the local paper. Let's not waste the stamp.' An understandable attitude, though it's not true when they say that to understand all is to forgive all!

Another reason why the titles of opportunities may be unfamiliar to you is that course organizers seem to take pleasure in devising original – and sometimes rather obscure – names for their returners' programmes. For example, your local college may offer 'Gateway', 'Fresh Horizons', 'Open Door', 'Return to Study', 'Second Chance', 'New Directions', 'Wider

Opportunities', 'Way In', 'Replan', 'Sampler', 'Threshold', 'New Beginnings', 'Drop-In Workshops', 'Pathway', 'Wider Horizons', 'Second Step for Women', 'Second Start', 'Managing a Career Break', 'Women on the Move', 'New Moves for Women' or 'Wider Access Programmes'. All these are titles of courses being offered in 1990 by individual colleges in England, Wales, Scotland and Northern Ireland, and they are simply courses designed to help you decide on your best direction and to prepare you for the appropriate training, on or off the job.

Once specific training opportunities have been established, the government's Employment Training scheme has limitless potential if you are able to take advantage of it. Among the new opportunities created by ET are retraining for a former woman civil servant to enter the travel trade (she's already been on a visit to Turkey as part of her training) and training for a 55-year-old who, after 30 years with British Coal, has taken a supervisory job in a plastics moulding factory.

COURSES ON COURSES
Generally speaking, anything with 'New', 'Fresh' or 'Wider' in the title is aimed at people who are not sure what opportunities exist for them and would value the chance to learn about their options. The original 'New Opportunities for Women' course was pioneered by Ruth Michaels at Hatfield Polytechnic. The idea was to offer a one-day-a-week course for ten weeks during school hours, in which women thinking of returning to work or retraining could learn about possible careers and courses and explore their own potential. The response was so overwhelming that in the first year the college had to run three courses instead of the planned one. Now there are around 50 'NOW' courses running in the UK.

There is no official syllabus for this sort of course, and some colleges may find it more practical to fit the programme of talks, discussions and (sometimes) aptitude tests into ten days, instead of ten weekly sessions. What you can be sure of is that you'll learn about local opportunities (very useful if you have home responsibilities which strictly limit your travel-to-work or travel-to-study area), national demand for particular qualifications (invaluable if you're starting out to get the exam passes that qualify you to enter a profession with a long training, like speech therapy or accountancy) and about how to cope with applications, enquiries, tests and interviews.

'Wider Opportunities' courses are often, though not always, funded as a preliminary to Employment Training. The government-sponsored versions are usually fitted neatly into a week, and often include sessions on assessing your abilities and potential. They often include skill-sampling opportunities as well as advice on job search and presentation for those who are interested in, and ready to apply for, vacancies. Again, advice is given to people who need further training on ways of getting it. At New College, Durham, women on the Wider Opportunities course 'have the chance to sample Computing, Catering, Office Technology, Sport, Art & Design, Music & Drama, Welding, Carpentry, Car Maintenance, Painting & Decorating, Bricklaying and Electrical Engineering. Sessions are also held on job-search skills and self-presentation'.

When you find the words 'Directions' or 'Horizons' in a course title, it could suggest that the organizers don't necessarily expect people who attend to have definitely decided to return to work. Some will be there just to discover whether or not it is a possibility. Others may have picked the course because they feel in need of some advice on which way to turn. At Somerset College of Arts and Technology I met a group which included widows and divorcees, recovering from the trauma of loss and still having to adjust to life alone, who had taken a 'New Directions' course because they felt it would help them cope with a different way of living. Don't ever feel that by taking an introductory course you are committing yourself to a particular course of action. As a spokesperson for Somerset College of Arts & Technology told me, 'The classic opportunity that we can give people is to identify their needs and get something done about them'. Most of these courses are specifically designed to show you the wide range of options available.

RETURN-TO-STUDY COURSES

You might think these are only for people who have previously studied and 'dropped out', but they are just as useful for people who didn't study beyond school-leaving age, as course organizers usually expect all students to need to learn modern methods of studying that make it easy to learn and to present your knowledge. For instance, the Shipley College course is 'specially designed for people without educational qualifications. They may have left school early, recently become unemployed or have been out of the job market for several years'. What you get, apart from learning job-search skills is 'a very basic introduction to the computer's role in the work-place . . . a chance to improve communication skills . . . individual counselling and plenty of opportunity for discussion in a friendly, relaxed atmosphere with like-minded adults and skilled staff'.

The 'Return to . . .' tag is very popular with colleges, but don't overlook anything entitled 'Pathway' or 'Gateway' as this too may indicate a fresh introduction to studying and an update on the latest methods. Some Return-to-Study courses are designed to prepare you for the next step – if you want to take it – on to an Access course.

COURSES THAT PROVIDE ENTRY QUALIFICATIONS

'Access' is the main title used for these courses, which are mostly designed to bring people up to the standard necessary to take a degree or Higher National Diploma course (though some are aimed at preparation for the training course of a particular profession, eg, Access to Nursing, Access to Social Work). There is a huge choice nationwide, and as I write this chapter of the book, I've just been invited to attend the press launch of the first *Access to Higher Education: Courses Directory*, published by ECCTIS/CNAA/FAST (this will help your local library track it down). The directory has been designed not only to list Access courses, but to say which subject areas they serve, how the course is timetabled, whether child care is available and where there are links with specific higher education providers. For example, South Warwickshire College of Further Education has links with Coventry Polytechnic and the University of Warwick; Guildford College of Technology's Access course has links with Kingston Polytechnic and the University of Surrey.

Access courses differ, but one student explained: 'We've studied English Literature, developing our skills of verbal and oral communication; Study Skills, which everybody on the course needed, and Maths . . . We've also touched on Psychology, Philosophy and some Sociology, and we've visited the polytechnic where we will be doing our degrees, for an introduction to each person's specialized subject.'

'Foundation' courses can provide a basic qualification on

which to build, eg, Accountancy Foundation, or they may be designed for people who have demonstrated their academic ability in one field and want to move into another. There are a number of HITECC Diploma Foundation courses for people who want to convert to science, engineering or technology. Typical is that offered by Nottingham Polytechnic, designed 'to provide people with a good working knowledge of Engineering Sciences, Maths and Computing'. The course leads directly into HNDs and polytechnic degrees in Computing, all types of Engineering, Mathematics and BEd courses in Mathematics & Sciences or Craft, Design & Technology. As a rule, HITECC courses don't expect any previous knowledge of Maths or Science beyond O-level.

EMPLOYMENT TRAINING

This is the latest government scheme to help people who want to return to work or start a new career. It is open to people over 18 and under 60 who have been unemployed for at least six months (so that lets in most returners). A special feature of ET, though, is that it aims to help people gain the skills and knowledge needed to compete for jobs in the local labour market. There is also provision made for people who want to set up in business on their own account – again locally in the first instance (your small business could be so successful that you establish branches nationwide).

There are good and bad things about the emphasis on local opportunities in the ET scheme. In the past, people were often financed to train for an occupation and then found that there were no local vacancies, nor any prospects of any. No-one wants to suggest that trainees should be forced into uncongenial work, but it's very disheartening, as well as a waste of time and money, to be trained for a job you have no hope of getting. The need for Jobcentres to be satisfied that there is a local demand for the skills sought under ET is common sense.

Also good is the fact that ET involves actual job experience as well as time at college in a programme designed to suit the needs of the individual. This helps to deal with the prejudice of employers who insist that you must have work experience before they can consider you – presumably experience gained at some other employers' expense! People with ET training should have a good balance of practical and theoretical training. ET programmes, wherever possible, are designed so that the people taking them also study for recognized qualifications.

The range of ET provisions is extensive, mirroring the variety of employment offered throughout the country. The Employment Training Agency at Kingston in Surrey lists 'construction, information technology, welding, knitting-machine repairs and English as a second language' among the skills taught at its Surbiton centre (all with the opportunity of practical work experience) and liaises with other accessible Training Agency centres to provide additional training opportunities, typically musical instrument making. ET providers take particular care to provide equal opportunities for both sexes (a £50-a-week child-care allowance for lone parents is available) and to cater for trainees with disabilities. Provision for trainees with disabilities is not concentrated on locally available facilities (though the local availability of jobs in still borne in mind). Four residential training colleges offer ET courses in fields as diverse as audio-visual technology, travel and tourism, desk-top publishing, quantity surveying, electronics and horticulture.

If you're contemplating self-employment, ET offers a whole range of training opportunities. The key word to look for in this case is 'Enterprise'. Typically, a Business Enterprise Programme will provide classroom sessions spread out over a five-week period covering topics like finance, marketing and market research. This could be followed by occupational training, if you find you need additional knowledge and skills to develop your business idea, and counselling sessions to help you discuss the progress of your plans.

An Enterprise Rehearsal can be arranged, whereby you can try out your business idea under the control of the local Training Manager. When you are ready to start, and provided you meet the official regulations for the scheme (details from your Jobcentre), you may also be eligible for the well-publicized Enterprise Allowance of £40 a week for 52 weeks to help you get your business established.

Like ET for jobs, ET for self-employment is free and you continue to receive any benefits to which you're already entitled, plus about £10 a week. There are also provisions to help anyone with high travel costs or who must take residential training.

The bad thing about ET is that it is only available for 'up to 12 months' (concessions allow longer training for people with disabilities). Up to 12 months can mean that in practice the authorities deem that you only need six months, or perhaps less, to get the skills you want and which *they* think will make you more employable. For many careers, the training normally lasts longer than 12 months, so despite the Jobcentre's best efforts to meet your personal needs, and the fact that you can demonstrate a demand for people with the proposed qualification and skill in your district, you may still be ineligible for ET. Alas, it can't be used as a way to finance that postgraduate course in arts administration for which you haven't been able to get a grant!

It's always worth asking your Jobcentre what schemes of training and retraining exist in your area. Schemes do change, as do the regulations governing them. Anyone who writes careers books can almost guarantee that his or her 'reviews' will comment that the government scheme(s) mentioned have been amended since the book was written.

CAREER DEVELOPMENT LOANS

These are an official success story. Piloted first in Aberdeen, Bristol/Bath, Greater Manchester and the Reading/Slough areas, they proved so successful that they are now available nationwide. Co-operation between three banks – Barclays, the Clydesdale and the Co-operative – provides sums from £500 to £5,000 to people who want to take a job training course and finance it themselves. (Sometimes, of course, it's not so much a case of *wanting* to finance it themselves as *having* to finance it themselves.)

The government pays the interest on the Career Development Loan during the period of training, and for up to three months afterwards, then you have to take over responsibility for repayment. Any course is eligible, provided it is job-related, lasts for at least one week and not more than a year, and does not attract a mandatory student award. Full-time, part-time, weekend and distance learning courses are included (so a typing course with the Open College or a programming course with the National Extension College would be eligible). You can also apply for a Career Development Loan if you want to take a course offered by a private college (such as the Morris Masterclass School of Hairdressing or the Cordon Bleu Cookery School). You can get a booklet with full details of this loan scheme from any Jobcentre, or any branch of one of the banks which provide the loans, or by ringing (free) 0800 585 505.

Three books that will help you track down possible courses on a nationwide basis are: *The Kogan Page Mature Students' Handbook* (Kogan Page), which deals specifically with opportunities and courses for people changing jobs or retraining; *The Directory of Further Education* (Hobsons/CRAC), which lists all courses offered at further education and some private colleges; and *DITTO – The Directory of Independent Training & Tutorial Organisations* (Trotman) listing private courses, from beauty therapy to pilot training. All are likely to be in your public library, though a version of *DITTO* was produced as five separate booklets, eg, *Getting Into Alternative Medicine, Getting Into Keep Fit & Beauty,* etc.

Books of this kind are as valuable for the ideas they might give you (would you have thought of stud and stable management or radiotherapy?) as for the course information that they provide. An hour in the library skimming through such material could be a valuable preliminary (or follow-up) to an 'opportunities' course, or even a substitute if you find it difficult to get to college.

MEMO TO EMPLOYERS

Colleges which run 'New Opportunities' or 'Return to Work' courses are often on the look-out for people who can give a talk to participants about the work they do. Whether you are a social worker or a supermarket manager, this is your chance to get your message across, not simply to the potential women returners on the course, but to the course organizers who may incorporate what you say into their regular programmes, or recommend you to other departments in the college as a knowledgeable lecturer. Opportunities to liaise with the Jobcentre in providing work experience for those on ET programmes are also worth taking. Just as employers who participate in YTS get the opportunity to observe young workers over a sustained period of training and offer permanent employment to the most promising ones, so ET gives you a chance to see how adult entrants can adapt to your style of working. You can regard the period of work training in ET as a very extended trial, almost certainly giving you a better idea of an individual's capabilities than you can gain from an interview. Both you and the employee have a chance to discover not only if she or he has the ability to learn the necessary skills for the job, but whether the potential new entrant would work well with your existing workforce.

CHAPTER 6

BRIDGING THE GAP

ARE YOU READY TO RETURN?

So many employers nowadays offer updating and retraining for women who are returning to work after a break that you may be in the fortunate position of not having to organize your own refresher course. An advertisement sparkling with enthusiasm appeared in the London *Evening Standard* during autumn 1989: a national chain of fashion stores sought women 'returning to work after a career break', willing to work 27–32 hours a week. They claimed that successful candidates who 'were unlikely to be under 22' would need the ability to motivate and lead people and have had some management or supervisory experience 'preferably in retail'. In return, they offered a first-class training programme, clothing allowance, discount provision, subsidized restaurant and five weeks' holiday a year. Plus salary, of course!

In the same newspaper was an advertisement from a knitting machine manufacturer who wanted demonstrators. 'Experience is preferred,' the advertiser specified, 'but as you would expect, full product training will be given, helping you to succeed quickly.' Someone with good hobby experience of using a knitting machine at home could have been ideal for that training.

Opportunities to retrain in employment multiply according to the demand for new blood in the workforce. Both the teaching and nursing professions provide numerous opportunities to gain new skills or to switch specialities during employment, so that if you manage to keep a toe-hold in your career, working, say as a 'bank' nurse or a supply teacher, you will be among the first to be considered for training opportunities.

Even after a career break, if you have had a sustained period of work experience before you gave up your job, there's a good chance of finding employers willing to update you as a paid employee when you are ready to return to work. It may not always be possible to restart at the level you left if there have been dramatic changes in systems and methods, because this could hold up the progress of a department. But provided you are fairly flexible about where you re-start, an undemanding job which can be handed over to another member of staff while you take time off to be coached in new techniques is quite a likely possibility. For an employer, it is cheaper to teach an experienced person some new skills than to have to train a beginner from scratch.

Although this sort of opportunity is particularly noted in service industries - shops, offices, catering - I've seen 'on the job' updating provided by a car manufacturer, who withdrew individual workers from the production line for retraining during their work shifts. Some were updating knowledge of electrical systems, others learning about computer-controlled production methods. They worked through individual teaching programmes at their own pace, using teaching videos, each trainee being provided with his or her own video machine. The tapes could be rewound and replayed whenever the trainee wished, so that there was no embarrassment of having to admit you found something tricky and needed to go over it again, and a tutor was available to give advice to anyone who sought it. People updating in this way commented that they found it far easier to learn new techniques at their own pace in this adult way than they remembered from their early training days in a group training centre when shyer people often hesitated to say they didn't understand something.

From the employer's point of view, it was an advantage to have the updating done on company premises, not only because it saved time, but because it meant that if a bottleneck or problem did occur on the production line while a particular worker was learning by video, he or she could be quickly recalled to sort it out, returning to the course later.

FINDING OUT ABOUT UPDATING
If you want or hope to return to a particular employer – the local authority, say, or a commercial group – it does no harm

to write and ask them for advice on the best updating course to take. You may well be invited for an interview to discuss the possibilities open to you and the changes that may have taken place since you last worked. This could be an advantage for many reasons: you have a chance to show what you remember of your previous experience and there might be an opportunity to discuss child-care arrangements if you have family responsibilities.

The employer can compare your past experience with the known demand for skills in the business and may well be able to recommend a specific course, a named qualification or a method of learning (perhaps an Open Learning package - see Chapter 7) that would cover all the new developments you'd need to know about in order to make a successful return. At the same time, you might learn about new kinds of job that have been created since you last worked. Some might appeal to you more than your original choice and you could direct your training in an appropriate way.

Perhaps, though, you've moved districts, and there is no one particular employer with which you have any contact? Then your Jobcentre could be helpful in telling you about local firms which might use the skills and knowledge you previously obtained. Also, if you are free to retrain full-time, they could help by suggesting Employment Training schemes for you. As explained in the previous chapter, these incorporate theoretical training with work experience.

If you are not yet ready to retrain full-time, a Jobcentre Adviser may be able to help by searching through the *Open Learning Directory* to locate a study package you could work through at home (again, see Chapter 7 for more details).

LOCAL PROVISION

In recent years, local authority further education colleges (and some schools of art and agriculture, too) have made a real effort to attract mature students by setting up refresher courses linked to local opportunities. Most popular are courses for returning secretaries – they may have titles like 'The Electronic Office' or 'Coping with Office Technology', or be simply called 'Secretarial Refresher'. If you're fortunate, such local courses may be organized during school hours and terms, but even if no such facility is available in your area, there is usually the alternative option of brushing up on a single subject, like shorthand, or joining a beginners' world-processing group in the evenings.

Similarly, 'Back to Nursing' courses are put on from time to time by colleges working in association with local hospitals. Often they're arranged so that the updating is spread over, say, a term, with attendance once or twice a week. You could update on nursing procedures, changes in health service systems and new drugs, for example. Usually, too, you get a chance to find out exactly what opportunities exist in your area, for part-time, weekend, sessional, bank or other schemes to use 'returners'.

Where you live may affect the sort of course established to attract women returners to new jobs. Proximity to Felixstowe, the second largest container port in the European Community, prompted Suffolk College of Higher & Further Education to put on three 32-week courses for women returners who wanted to train as customs clearance specialists. They learned German or French, computer software systems, international trade and payments and import and export administration, ending up with a BTEC Certificate in Business Administration (Importing and Exporting). This is the sort of innovative course you are likely to find out about by making enquiries at the local Jobcentre, since living close to the job is one of the probable entry requirements for training.

Some colleges offer short courses to people who want to re-enter the job market and take advantage of local demand. They are not confined to those who want to work for an employer: for instance, if you're a farmer's wife, thinking about the possibility of taking holiday visitors, it's worth asking if the local agricultural college has a 'Farm Tourism' course, or whether the further education college offers a 'Running a Bed and Breakfast' programme. 'Managing a Newsagency' and 'Your Own Dressmaking Business' are other subjects that have been offered on a short course basis.

SINGLE SUBJECT UPDATING
It's worth mentioning at this stage that many polytechnics – it seems to be a poly speciality – have a scheme whereby you can become an 'Associate Student'. This means you can pick out one element of a degree or higher diploma course that you may feel you need to know more about, and just pay to attend those lectures each week. It could be anything from quantitative

methods to social psychology and you usually have the choice of doing coursework and taking an assessment at the end of the session.

If you do the coursework and have it and your assessment marked, then (a) you have something to show a future employer as evidence of your up-to-the minute knowledge, or (b) you may decide to use this achievement as the foundation for further study, and take other parts of the course on a part-time or full-time basis, ending with the appropriate degree or diploma. This sort of approach may give you the extra opportunity of being able to change the direction of your career when you are ready to return to work.

PROFESSIONAL UPDATING

If you hold a professional qualification or have graduate status, you may be lucky and find a 'Professional Updating for Women' course run at a local polytechnic. Hatfield Polytechnic (which initiated the 'New Opportunities for Women' courses) is among a small number of colleges running these school-hours only courses which cater for professionally-qualified women who need help in re-entering the world of work. The Hatfield course includes work experience in each participant's field, as well as an overview of developments that affect many professional occupations, such as computerization. Individual professional institutes, discussed later in this chapter, may run their own intensive updating courses on a residential, fee-paying basis (see page 54).

OPEN UNIVERSITY

Though Chapter 7 concentrates on distance-learning methods of training and retraining, it is worth emphasizing in this chapter that the Open University's Continuing Education provision includes many courses that can be taken at home as a way of bridging the gap between old and new employment, to inform returners about techniques and systems that may have been introduced since they last worked. They publish a free guide to 'Open Opportunities', covering all the areas of knowledge in which these updating courses are offered.

Perhaps you are a returning teacher? One of the computing education programmes might be helpful, such as 'Micros in schools project: a programme of microcomputer education packs for teachers'. A special 'Mathematics Update' project was also introduced by the OU in 1988 as their contribution to increasing the supply of mathematics teachers, urgently needed in the profession. Distance-learning provision to cater for special needs revealed in particular occupations is a feature of the OU's Continuing Education programmes.

Among dozens of management courses, you'll find 'Accounting and Finance for Managers' and 'International Marketing', while the health and social welfare range of courses includes 'Mental Health problems in old age', providing a valuable insight into problems and provisions for doctors, nurses, social workers, paramedical workers and all those whose careers involve them in working with elderly people.

COLLEAGUES AND CONTACTS

A very good source of advice on updating courses are professional and trade organizations. For instance, the Law Society can put you in touch with the Association of Women Solicitors, and the Royal Institute of British Architects has a Women Architects' Group. Most occupations have a professional institute, a trade union or an employers' organization. One of their primary responsibilities will be to encourage new entrants to the career concerned, and increasingly, these organizations are sponsoring, financing or publicizing short courses which can be taken by people wishing to brush up on the latest developments in their field. Libraries stock the *Directory of British Associations* which lists professional, trade, commercial and employers' associations with their addresses and phone numbers – a good starting point for enquiries about women's groups and/or refresher courses.

You do usually have to take the initiative and write to the organization concerned to ask what is available. If your organization has a members' magazine, and if you've continued to subscribe to it, you'll find that courses for returners are often publicized there. Some courses, though not specifically for people who have taken a career break, may cover new methods or materials being used in the career. Though aimed at people at work, the information could be a valuable way to update for anyone thinking of making a return. For instance, after taking such a course, at a job interview you might ask, 'Are TVEI courses being offered in the school?' or 'Does this hospital use the cook-chill meals system?' Showing you are aware of developments in your career area demonstrates clearly that you have not been so preoccupied at home that you have become out of touch with the working world, particularly as far as it affects the probable content of your own return to work.

To be financially viable, most updating courses have to be set up in a centre that is accessible to a large number of potential applicants for places. That usually means Inter-City locations such as Birmingham, Manchester, London, Glasgow or Bristol. Because such courses are aimed at a national audience, they are almost inevitably residential. Course organizers realize that people who are paying their own expenses can't afford long hotel stays (nor may it be possible to leave the family for more than a few days), so the most likely format is to offer a short, very intensive course, backed up by lots of take-away course material that you can revise in your own time.

If you've been away from learning for a long time, then before you invest money in an intensive career update, it's not a bad idea to take a study-skills course, either at a local college or by distance learning (see Chapter 7). This is a bit like booking a few lessons on the local dry ski slope before you go off to the mountains for intensive ski instruction. It gets you into the habit of note-taking, skimming books and learning to express yourself succinctly so that you will get more out of your professional update.

Courses run by professional, trade and employer organizations may only be offered once or twice a year, so you do need to keep looking out for them. It would be uneconomic to advertise this sort of course in national newspapers, so keep an eye on special-interest magazines, institute newsletters or house magazines, as appropriate for your career.

When you contact a professional association, employers group or trade union, you may discover that it has a separate arm for women members, or is in touch with a support group that women have set up for themselves. Occupational groups range from 'Women in Banking' to 'Women in Physics'. The book *Returning to Work* from the Women Returners' Network includes a list of current support groups, but if your career choice doesn't feature, write anyway to your occupation's national organization (see the *Directory of British Associations*). There may be one in the pipeline.

EMPLOYMENT AGENCIES

One of the most interesting developments in past years has been the provision of 'cross-training' by those office employment agencies which have made a speciality of supplying word-processing operators. Individual computer manufacturers commonly produce word-processing programs that are unique to their own machines, so that, for example, someone trained on an Apple Macintosh computer might need to learn a different system if faced by an Apricot or an Olivetti. Because people with secretarial skills are much in demand, it pays agencies to provide short updating courses on their premises so that returning secretaries can learn new systems. Where it's not feasible to provide on-the-spot training, an agency may have close links with local colleges, and be able to recommend specific refresher courses to meet an individual returner's needs. Specially-trained counsellors can assess a job applicant's existing skills and recommend a good source for any updating needed.

Commercial, catering and industrial employment agencies are the most widely available nationwide, but there are also independent agencies which cater for occupations as diverse as paramedical professionals and sales representatives. The Federation of Recruitment and Employment Services is an organization representing independent employment agencies in the UK and has a *Yearbook of Recruitment and Employment Services* (Longman) listing them, classified both according to region and the type of job vacancies they handle. This is one of the more expensive reference books (£27.50 including postage and packaging), so (a) it's not necessarily republished annually and (b) you are most likely to find it in a big public library.

Because employment agencies only get paid by the employers whose staff requirements they satisfy, and not by the would-be employees they interview and counsel, they can be a very useful source of assessment and advice to the returner. Their income depends on their ability to find people with the skills in demand from employers, so they are in a strong position to tell you what is needed at the time you approach them. Don't expect them to be long-term career counsellors, though. Their interest is in supplying current needs, and it's their advice on the most useful skills to acquire for a rapid return to work that will be most useful.

DO-IT-YOURSELF UPDATING
Of course, the ideal time to work out how you are going to keep in touch is *before* you give up your job. Perhaps, as time goes by and employers realize that they can't really afford to let their experienced younger staff leave to raise families or care for relatives without making some effort to keep their loyalty, pre-career-break schemes will be launched.

This is a lot easier in some occupations than in others. For instance, journalists and publishing staff are often encouraged to take on freelance reporting or editing during a career break. Teachers and lecturers can do evening work or the occasional session of 'supply' or home teaching. In manufacturing areas like clothing, outworkers can make up garments at home. In the service industries, caterers often take on tasks like preparing canapes and cocktail snacks at home, or will specialize in something like directors' lunches, which can be conveniently fitted into school hours. In fact, they never really take a 'career break'.

Some enterprising women actually use their career break to develop their career reputation. I've listened with interest to one radio producer who has timetabled features on pregnancy, types of delivery, baby care, coping with toddlers and first days at school over the last six years. Now when I turn on my radio, I hear she's back into mainstream broadcasting, presenting programmes that fit neatly into school hours. Would that we were all so forward-thinking and organized!

All the same, many occupations could lend themselves to adaptation so that the career gap can be bridged in such a way that on a CV it looks as if you've never been out of touch. Perhaps you've been a sales representative? Could you become a manufacturers' agent, working from home, and mainly by phone, representing an overseas client? Could you teach selling skills at a local college evening class? Could you write for a sales or trade magazine? How about telesales from your own home?

If you can't use your specific skills and qualifications on a paid basis, you may be able to 'keep your hand in' as a voluntary worker. Charities and campaigning groups more often than not exist on the spare-time help given by people with full-time jobs or full-time domestic commitments. If you can help with the accounts or by acknowledging donations – work you can do at home – or if you can participate in a different way, say using your communication skills to talk to women's groups about your campaign or organizing a local collection, this is yet another way of keeping in touch with the world outside your own four walls. If you've held down a high-powered job, it may seem little enough to do, but it does help to bridge the gap between your former working life and your current domestic commitments, and you'll have less difficulty adjusting to a work environment and conversations on topics that have nothing to do with the responsibilities of your private life.

Many people, particularly women caring for dependent relatives, have to face the fact that they'll be taking an involuntary career break with little chance to 'bridge the gap' by attending classes or meetings or taking home-based courses. As the percentage of elderly people in the population increases, many more women may find themselves detached from the working community and joining the band of 'carers'.

Though relief from the 24-hour responsibility may be possible through a local volunteer group or, if you're lucky, through the help of a carer from the local authority team, probably the last thing you will want to do with your free time is update on your career. No-one would blame you for wanting to use your limited time off simply for relaxation, gossip with friends, a trip to the library or a meal that you haven't had to prepare.

There may be times when you're 'on duty', however, when you can contrive to provide yourself with an adaptable kind of updating, designed and organized to suit you. Taking a magazine concerned with your career interests is one way of keeping in touch. You may find yourself reading it in the small hours, but you will feel less detached if you know what's going on in the working world that once was yours. Even more useful could be the introduction of a video recorder to your lifestyle. You can tape programmes (or sometimes, courses) and watch them when you get a free moment. Many distance-learning courses (see Chapter 7) also incorporate videotape instruction.

Whatever your reason for having a career break, if you are able to keep in touch with people still working in your field, do make every effort to do so. It isn't just that this will alert you to changes taking place in your workplace, or even that it's valuable to have contacts with people employed in your career speciality, who may one day be able to recommend you for a job when you are able to return to work. The interpretation of work changes: how people are adjusting, the kind of efforts being made by employers to retrain staff and, often, stories of problems people have overcome in adopting new methods, are all useful to know about, so that you never feel totally 'detached' from the world of work. Listen out for the anecdotes that will help you avoid problems encountered by other people. Take an interest in work gossip – it's often educational. And always be on the lookout for newspaper reports, magazine articles, radio and TV programmes and college courses that relate to your past (or maybe your future) career. Career awareness is something everyone can develop, and at job interviews it is often a factor that decides who the selectors feel has shown the greatest interest in the work being offered.

MEMO TO EMPLOYERS
The best way to bridge the career gap from your point of view is not to let it happen! When a valuable employee announces that she's leaving to start a family or leaving to take on some other demanding domestic responsibility, make sure she knows she will be welcome to re-apply for work if she finds she has time available, and mention any opportunities there might be for sessional work (eg, lunch-time relief or casual work at sale time). If there is any work that can be done at home, it is obviously helpful to mention this, too. In the excitement of starting a new kind of life at home, the value of having an employer who would welcome you back may be overlooked. So see if it's possible to compile a set of notes that can accompany the final pay cheque.

You will want to dream up your own version, but the theme might be 'Leaving Work? We'd like to keep in touch'. In the notes you could mention any benefits you offer ex-employees (such as first chance of sessional work, as mentioned above), the opportunity to get the company newsletter or magazine, any links you have with local colleges for updating courses. You could suggest ways of keeping up to date – perhaps, if yours is a professional service, there are seminars for members of professional institutes, or a trade magazine to recommend. If there is any opportunity for your former worker to revisit you, do mention this. Hospitals and factories are among the environments where all-comers are welcomed to Open Days. Free or concessionary entry could be attractive to former employees.

As part of your overall plan to attract former employees, make sure your Personnel or Recruitment Officer is aware of any opportunities for skills updating offered through Jobcentres or local colleges, and follows up any advertisements for independent training centres or distance-learning provision of updating courses so that possible returners get a friendly, positive, informative response to any enquiry they may make.

CHAPTER 7

LEARNING AT HOME

The traditional picture of a correspondence course student at work shows her seated comfortably at the dining room table with a standard lamp at her elbow and a crackling fire in the background. Absorbed in her work, with an interesting-looking pile of books beside her, she's writing pages of notes, clearly in a fascinating world of her own. Only a cynic would take a wider-angled view of this scene – showing the children quarrelling over which TV channel to watch while their father is moodily poking holes in the cling-film covering his choice of DIY microwave supper.

Before you get carried away by the thought of working at your own pace in your own place, you must consider exactly when and how you will study, particularly if you already have a full working life. If it is already impossible for you to spare time to attend classes, how are you going to make time to learn at home?

The successful completion of a distance-learning course depends a great deal on organization and self-discipline. For example, you can look for times to study when you don't have the family around you – before they get up, for instance. Lots of people must do this, otherwise the Open University would not schedule pre-breakfast TV courses. If you commute to work, you can read textbooks on the train – a very successful study group was established on the Cambridge to London commuter line some years ago. While the washing whirls round in the launderette; while the rest of the family watch *Match of the Day*; while you're making the kind of casserole that instructs you to 'stir from time to time' – you can make enough time for a study course.

As you get into the habit of studying again, and provided you've chosen the right subject and level, you could well find you're just as happy getting on with your course as watching TV or reading a library book. It is stimulating and satisfying to discover that you're doing well, and when you have an objective in view – meeting the entrance requirements for a chosen career, for instance – you'll feel you are really making progress when you find words of praise from your tutor on returned work.

Once you are at this stage, working on your course becomes a treat rather than a task to be fitted in with everything else and you will find yourself planning what you are going to say in your next essay as you walk to the shops, or promising yourself another look at the course video when you are doing the ironing.

Many of the people who decide to investigate home-study courses do so because they have not enjoyed learning in a group at school. Certainly if you feel apprehensive about re-starting a study course among strangers who may know more than you, it's an easy way to test your abilities. Unless you are aiming at a specific examination on a specific date, you really can work at your own pace.

If you don't understand at the first attempt, you can keep re-reading the course material until you do – or you can write to your tutor with your problem. Meanwhile, none of the other distance-learning students taking your course will know that you've had difficulties with it, any more than you will know how well they are doing. At the same time, of course, you don't have any competition to spur you on; your objective has to be simply to get better results each time you return an assignment.

TUTORIALS

Many providers of distance-learning courses now offer telephone tutorials or face-to-face meetings with tutors as an optional extra. Will it help in your case to be able to ring up your tutor if you get stuck with an assignment – or to visit a college by arrangement for a discussion of your course work?

A lot may depend on the course you take. Something that is primarily learned by printed lessons, textbooks and written assignments may be fairly easily taught in the same way. Something that involves practical work could well prove easier to learn if you have the opportunity to see demonstrations from time to time. The development of course materials that include videotapes and computer programs makes it a lot easier to teach practical skills, and in many parts of the country, distance-learning students can arrange to book time at a local college's 'drop in' centre, where they can use the video machines or computers to study their own courses. When you are enquiring about distance-learning courses, ask if this is available in your area and how much it costs to book a session at the centre.

A special feature of Open University undergraduate courses is that students are expected to attend summer schools where they meet tutors (and each other) and take part in seminars and discussions, or, depending on the course, watch demonstrations or use high-tech equipment not available outside a university or polytechnic. Some local education authorities offer financial help with the cost of attending summer school – find out if yours is one of them.

STAYING THE COURSE

Start with a course that you feel you can manage comfortably. For example, if you must have GCSE Maths for the career of your choice and you failed it at school, you'd probably do better to begin with something like the National Extension College's 'Access to Maths', described as, 'An introductory course to all of you who were afraid of maths at school. It is also a good revision course if you are returning to maths and need to brush up your skills. If you enjoy the course, you can be reasonably confident that you can go on to GCSE Maths.'

The same college also offers 'Access to English', 'Access to History', 'Access to Human Biology' and 'Access to Physics', as well as a range of 'How to Study' courses. It's true that nothing succeeds like success: once you do manage to complete a distance-learning course successfully, you'll probably be hooked on independent learning, because in the process of taking your course, you have developed the skill of self-directed study.

A trap to avoid is taking on too much. Commonly, people read that they need five GCSEs or three A-levels for their next level of career preparation, and are often tempted to tackle the entire batch at once and 'get it over with'. It's wiser to settle for, say, two GCSEs or just one A-level and give yourself adequate time to prepare for the exam(s), remembering that you are learning a new method of studying as well as tackling a new subject.

As a useful guide to how long you might need to study for a particular course, see if the local further education college offers it. If they set aside two three-hour lecture sessions a week plus study time, you can appreciate that you're not going to be able to jam two A-levels into the spaces available when your toddler is at playgroup and when you also have to cope with the shopping, washing, ironing, etc.

If you do find that it's all much easier than you expected, I promise you that the correspondence college will be only too delighted to enrol you for additional subjects! An advantage of distance learning is that you don't have to wait for the academic year to start in September to begin a course. You can enrol at any time of year and, as you set the pace of learning, you may find you can reach examination standard more quickly than the average person learning in a group.

CHOICE OF COURSES

It is now possible to study almost every subject by distance learning methods, from introductory English and basic Arithmetic, through pre-GCSE and on to GCSE and A-levels, continuing to degree and even postgraduate levels.

In addition to these academic courses, there are vocational distance-learning packages for every kind of occupation and interest, from computing to freelance writing, electronics to touch-typing. Experimental kits, audio and video-tapes, plus access to technical equipment through selected colleges makes it possible for home-based students to watch demonstrations and develop practical skills by following instructions on a video or computer screen.

The national Open College specializes in courses that teach specific job skills – caring, selling, typing, information technology, etc. The Open College of the Arts provides home-study tuition in subjects like painting, photography, sculpture, textiles and art and design.

If you want to work for yourself, you can take a small business course or choose, from a wide range of business subjects, those that you think would be particularly useful to you. Perhaps you need to learn book-keeping or brush up on selling skills? You might pick out a specialized course like 'Running a Shop' or work towards a specific qualification such as a BTEC Certificate of Achievement (Marketing).

If you want to return to your former profession but feel you may be out of touch with the latest methods and developments, there are also updating courses available by distance-learning in fields like nursing, micro-electronics and pharmacy. Professional institutes are usually knowledgable about this kind of provision and will direct you to an appropriate college. Some combine home-study packages with attendance at weekend seminars where you get the chance to meet other returners.

For people seeking professional qualifications, there is a very wide range of distance-learning courses. Among the qualifications you can study for by post are those of the Institute of Personnel Management, Institute of Health Services Management, Royal Town Planning Institute and Association of Accounting Technicians. Though it's not usually possible to qualify by examinations alone, having made a start on an appropriate course shows employers that you are serious in your intention to enter the career concerned, and will encourage them to offer you employment so that you can satisfy the 'practical experience' requirement.

The Open College has concentrated on courses that give people work skills, so their prospectus includes effective selling, learning to type, caring skills and book-keeping, as well as advanced courses like multi-disciplinary engineering which can be studied to either City & Guilds or BTEC Higher levels. There is also a wide range of business-related courses. Many further education colleges are access centres for the Open College, providing tutorial help or access to equipment such as computers.

The Open University is best known for its undergraduate degree courses which are open to all comers on a 'first come, first served' basis. You build up your degree by accumulating credits for each study package you complete. Most people begin with a foundation course, though you may gain exemptions from subjects you have already studied and passed. A feature of OU degree courses is that if you have to stop studying for a while – say, if your husband is posted abroad, or you are promoted into a new and demanding job which takes all your time – you can re-start just where you left off and complete your degree when it suits you.

An OU degree is worth exactly the same as a degree from any other university, and entitles you to apply for any job or training scheme that demands 'graduate status'.

In addition to undergraduate courses, the Open University runs a wide range of postgraduate courses, continuing education courses and the Open Business School which offers both individual subject courses, eg, Accounting or Marketing, plus DMS and MBA courses. Many returners are likely to be interested in the OU's range of continuing education courses. Former nurses can update by taking the course 'A Systematic Approach to Nursing Care' which explains the nursing process now adopted by the profession. Those with programming experience might well be interested in 'Introduction to Systems Analysis and Design'. The National Extension College offers 'Continuing Education for Pharmacists', and registered pharmacists who take this course can reclaim their course fee from the Department of Social Security via their Regional Pharmaceutical Officer.

In addition to all these sources of distance-learning, individual further education colleges frequently have specialized provision for 'open learning'. The *Open Learning Directory* lists more than 1,500 courses available by distance-learning. If it is not in your public library, ask your local Jobcentre for access to a copy.

To supply a college with all the equipment needed for specialist study of a particular occupation can be expensive, so you'll often find that within a county or region, one specific college will be the allocated centre for courses (including distance-learning materials) related to a named occupation. For example, Watford College, Hertfordshire has an Open Access centre with special provision for students of the printing, publishing and ink industries, as well as a more general provision of learning packages in fields like computing and electronics. Perth College of Further Education in Scotland provides individual learning packages in association with the Hotel & Catering Industry Training Board, the Road Transport Industry Training Board and the Seafish Industry Authority. In the North-West of England, Southport College of Art and Technology even offers its open learning 'Guest House Owner's' course with the option of tutorial back-up on the student's own premises if required.

Generally speaking, if your area is noted for a particular kind of industry, such as clothing manufacture, catering and tourism, micro-electronics or agriculture, you should find that there is a source of distance-learning courses based in some central location – often a college which also provides conventional day and evening courses. At these Open Learning centres, you can buy a learning package and also make arrangements to use facilities at the centre either on a 'drop in' basis, or by booking time on a computer, video or other equipment related to your course.

EMPLOYERS' ATTITUDES

If you obtain qualifications by distance learning, whether you're offering GCSEs, vocational certificates or a degree, you show potential employers two valuable qualities. First, you have been so strongly motivated to meet their entry requirements that you have paid for your own course and studied in your own time to meet their standards. Second, and even more important to most employers, you have shown that you have the self-discipline to work unsupervised, with the ability to timetable your own studies and set your own targets. These are intrinsic abilities that will be valued in any kind of job and may be specifically demanded for careers where you have to take early responsibility, such as nursing or social work.

Motivation, self-discipline and self-reliance are valuable qualities in any employee. So when you write your CV, make it clear that you obtained your qualifications by independent study. It all helps to give employers an idea of your personality.

COUNTING THE COSTS

At the time of writing, a typical GCSE English course including 52 activities and 15 tutor-marked assignments cost £125, with the possibility of a reduced fee for advance payment. In comparing costs with those charged for college-based courses, bear in mind that you have no travel expenses with the distance-learning course as all materials are sent to your home, and that you are being offered individual rather than group tuition.

Among updating courses, the 'Continuing Education for Pharmacists' course was offered at £25 for three study units and the 'Systematic Approach to Nursing' course on the nursing process also for approximately £25 for a workbook, case studies and audio tape.

The Open College charged £49.95 for its course in 'Effective

Selling', which comprised a video tape, audio tape and three workbooks. For a complete 'Small Business' course, the National Extension College charged £70, which covered the provision of 11 study units and seven tutor-marked assignments.

For a degree with the Open University, assuming that the student was not entitled to any exemptions, getting the six full credits and attending the required minimum of two summer schools cost £1,360 at 1989 rates. A foundation course leading to an OU credit cost up to £186 plus £122 for attendance at summer school, to which, as already mentioned, some local authorities will make a contribution.

Some employers not only encourage their staff to improve qualifications and prospects by taking distance-learning courses, but also contribute to fees. For anyone who is considering returning to or making a fresh start in the public service, it is worth noting that NALGO (the National and Local Government Officers' Association) offers a discount on standard correspondence course fees for subjects as diverse as professional qualifications, BTEC vocational qualifications and A-levels.

It is in your own interests to compare the tutorial methods, course content and costs of a range of distance-learning providers when there are several offering the subject you want to study. The most expensive course is not necessarily the best, though you should take into account options like being able to borrow a tape-recorder or being provided with a keyboard for practice instead of having to travel to a college to use its equipment. If in doubt, take advice from a professional institute or trade union, or from Jobcentre staff. Check that any course provider is accredited by the Council for the Accreditation of Correspondence Colleges.

MEMO TO EMPLOYERS

Always be positive in your response to prospective job applicants who may write to you enquiring about vacancies. If they lack the skills you need, and you know that those skills are taught either at a further education college or through a home study course, it's fair to say something like, 'From time to time, we recruit trainee technicians with GCSE/A-level Maths and Physics or an appropriate BTEC qualification. Though we cannot offer employment to everyone who applies with these qualifications, chances of a job are much greater for candidates who have reached this standard. You may like to investigate the courses offered by [names of local and distance-learning colleges].'

If you are a training provider (school of nursing, physiotherapy, radiography, etc), it may save you time to prepare an information sheet about entry requirements that gives details of any pre-entry or Access courses on offer, as well as mentioning the possibility of obtaining necessary GCSE/A-levels by distance-learning or at college. Mature entrants and returners often feel at a disadvantage compared to applicants from schools and colleges. By including in your careers literature some mention of distance-learning courses that can be taken by home-study, you show that you cater for candidates who want to prepare for a new career while raising a family. This will encourage them to approach you when they are free to return to work.

The Training Agency's Learning Systems and Access Branch can send you a list of Open Learning sources of help and advice – centres which can advise you about the courses available, to retrain an existing workforce, update returners or recommend to potential employees.

CHAPTER 8

RETRAINING FROM SCRATCH

For some potential returners, the experience of managing a home efficiently and creating a happy lifestyle can have a very positive effect on their personality. If you have developed a new confidence since you have been managing your own home in your own way, it's quite likely that you won't be content to return to what may well have been a safe but boring little groove in the employment market. You may want to make a fresh start in a career that will use the skills you have discovered you possess as a result of having to manage your home independently.

EMPLOYMENT PROSPECTS

In theory, if you have the academic entry requirements, meet age specifications and health criteria, there is nothing to stop you training for any new career. You could be an accountant or an ambulance driver, a chiropodist or a computer programmer, a solicitor or a surveyor. In practice, it is important to enquire into your employment prospects before you sign up for any course of training.

Quite often, training authorities themselves point out the importance of this. The Northern College of Chiropody, at Salford College of Technology, says: 'We have no upper age limit for students, but point out the potential employment problems for people who will be 50+ on qualification.' The Manchester School of Therapy Radiography says: 'We would have to think very carefully about accepting anyone over 45 years of age because of the high cost of the training and the candidate's potential working life as a radiographer then being only a maximum of 17 years.'

In occupations where there is considerable competition for entry, such as law, journalism, accountancy and advertising, making yourself eligible for training by passing appropriate exams does not guarantee a placement for practical training, but it can help you to establish a good working relationship with a prospective employer before you apply for a training course.

For example, someone who wants to become a journalist will stand a better chance if she becomes known as a reliable freelance contributor to magazines and newspapers. The would-be solicitor is more likely to be offered articles by a firm where her competence as a legal secretary or legal executive is known.

During pre-course interviews, most training authorities ask candidates if they have considered their prospects of employment. Alternatively, you can ask an interview panel if they have had previous mature entrants and how easily they obtained jobs on qualification. If in doubt, always seek an opinion from the appropriate professional institute or trade association.

MOBILITY

This applies to both training opportunities and employment prospects. For example, there is currently a considerable shortage of speech therapists – a profession in which maturity can be an asset and where most training centres will consider candidates aged up to 45 (50 in a few cases). However, there are only 14 universities/polytechnics/colleges in the UK offering the three- or four-year first degree, and just one providing a two-year postgraduate diploma. Unless you live within easy reach of one of these centres, the availability of job vacancies is irrelevant.

As I write, the newspapers are full of stories highlighting the country's shortage of primary schoolteachers. Almost daily there are reports of children being sent home because there are no teachers for them, or of local authorities seeking to recruit teachers from elsewhere in the ECC or the Commonwealth to make up the shortfall. 'But', said a spokesperson from the 'Teaching as a career unit' at the Department of Education and Science, 'it does depend on where you live. Whereas in Inner London, primary schoolteachers may take their pick of jobs, in, say, Cheshire, they'd be lucky to find a vacancy.'

You can see how important it is to check up on the demand

for newly qualified people as well as on the availability of training facilities when you are deciding on a second career. Jobcentre advisers and careers office staff who are constantly in touch with local employers will certainly be able to give you an idea of the situation in your particular area, while you can get the national picture from the relevant professional institute or trade association.

SECOND CHOICES
Unlike teenagers, who tend to say, 'I want to be an animal nurse' or 'I want to be a lawyer' and discourage any alternative suggestions, adults choosing new careers are more likely to look for certain qualities in the kind of work they want to train for. Adults will say, 'I want to work with people' or 'I want to work in a hospital' or 'I want to be my own boss'.

The COIC careers guide, *Occupations*, makes a special mention of 'related occupations' in each one of its career outlines. So this is a good source of ideas if you have a general idea of the work you'd like to do and want to consider various options.

The range of careers where new routes are being opened up to mature entrants tends towards the labour-intensive rather than capital-intensive. Where the work done by a person can be equally well done by a machine, opportunities are much fewer.

On the other hand, technology has made some jobs more interesting. The secretary with a word-processor can set up the agenda for a conference on her VDU, press the print key and leave the machine to get on with it while she discusses accommodation, menus and seminar equipment with the local hotel's conference manager. In the medical laboratory, routine analysis is done by machine, leaving the more interesting and specialized investigations for the scientific staff. Librarians use computer databases to control their stock and research queries put to them by visitors. Such developments may mean that your original career choice may be very different in content than your image of it, so it's valuable to talk about the work with someone currently doing the job, or getting advice on job content from an appropriate professional institute or training centre.

SOME LATE-START POSSIBILITIES
The selection of retraining ideas that follows is confined to

careers where maturity is generally regarded as an asset, sometimes a necessity, and where late-starters are normally welcomed. It is *not* exhaustive: as the supply of available school- and college-leavers diminishes, the governing bodies of many more occupations may seek to attract older entrants, and will probably provide entry concessions or special retraining schemes for them. Keep an eye on the education, employment and recruitment pages of the national press for this kind of opportunity.

WORK WITH CHILDREN AND IN EDUCATION

Nursery nursing

Though commonly taken up by young people who want to be nannies, this training also qualifies people to work in (or manage) day nurseries, run workplace crèches, work in nursery schools alongside nursery teachers and in hospital maternity units. An experienced nursery nurse could also set up her own day nursery in accordance with the regulations of the 1948 Nurseries and Child Minders Act (the Social Services Department will give advice on this).

Training for the National Nursery Examination Board's certificate lasts two years and is college-based with substantial periods of work experience in different child-care environments. There are a few extended three-year courses aimed at mature students who can attend during school hours only, and it is possible that as the demand for nursery care increases, as more firms seek to employ women returners, so colleges will respond by putting on more school-hours only courses, to train women who want to make a second career in nursery care. Experience with children is valuable, but as far as academic entry requirements are concerned, colleges can set their own standards. Generally, from two to five GCE or GCSE passes would be expected. Upper age limits are individual to colleges, but those which have offered extended courses have tended to take people aged up to about 45.

Information   National Nursery Examination Board, 8 Chequer Street, St Albans AL1 3XZ (Tel: 0727 47636).

Teaching

The experience of bringing up a family prompts many women to consider teaching as a possible second career. Apart from the fact that hours and holidays are likely to coincide, an interest in teaching often develops in women who have been encouraged to take an active part in children's education, helping out at nursery classes, sharing after-school activities, organizing fund-raising events, perhaps serving as school governors or managing a parent–teacher group.

For most age groups and subjects, candidates are considered up to the age of about 40 to 45, and for 'shortage' subjects, over-45s may be welcomed, particularly if they have a sound background of work in the subject concerned.

Graduates (mainly those with degrees in subjects that feature on the school timetable) may take one-year Postgraduate Certificate in Education courses to qualify to teach any age group in state schools, from nursery to secondary. At present there are one or two part-time two-year PGCE courses, but advisers at the 'Teaching as a career unit' remind women with family commitments that most full-time postgraduate courses only require part of the time to be spent at lectures or on teaching practice while other work can be done at home.

Twelve pilot projects in districts from Devon to North Yorkshire start in September 1990 whereby graduates may be trained as 'articled teachers'. Their paid two-year training will be 80 per cent work-based, with supervision from senior teachers in their schools and staff from nearby training colleges. 355 of the places available will be for primary education and the 175 remaining divided between secondary subjects like maths, modern languages, science, religious studies, business studies and craft, design and technology.

Non-graduate entrants to teaching must usually – though not invariably – have five O-levels and two A-levels, and normally take either the four-year Bachelor of Education degree course, or a degree in the subject they want to teach followed by the PGCE (see above). Colleges vary in the range of age groups they cater for and the subjects which prospective teachers may choose as major and minor interests. The *Handbook of Degree and Advanced Courses* (Lund Humphries) indicates which colleges offer which courses.

Many colleges offer substantial entry concessions to mature

students and will accept alternatives to GCE A-levels, such as the successful completion of an Access course, a BTEC course or Open University credits. The *Educational Credit Transfer Handbook* (ECCTIS) gives details of all these concessions and of shortened BEd courses for people whose qualifications are in great demand.

A problem often faced by those who want to train for teaching is the discovery that they must have English and Maths O-level/GCSE among their examination passes. This frequently frustrates people who are otherwise experienced and qualified for teacher training. One woman wrote: 'I have been assisting in the teaching of drama at the local comprehensive school for several years now, but, having failed Maths O-level four times, I despair of ever being able to qualify as a teacher.' Colleges, too, are aware of the problem. At the North London Polytechnic, student teachers are accepted provisionally for BEd degree courses without O-level Maths, and the polytechnic puts on summer coaching courses to help them pass the examination. If Maths O-level is an obstacle to your teaching career, ask your nearest teacher training college and the local FE college if they offer anything similar, and bear in mind the possibilities of being tutored through a distance-learning course (see Chapter 7).

If you have professional or technical qualifications or a degree in a useful subject, you may be able to pass on your knowledge by teaching in adult education, for which formal teaching qualifications are not necessary. Evening classes, sessional day work or even full-time employment may be possible.

You can also study for teaching qualifications in secretarial subjects or take the City & Guilds Further Education Teacher's Certificate course. The Royal Society of Arts and Trinity College, London examine for qualifications in 'Teaching English as a Foreign (or Second) Language'. Most professions have facilities for members to obtain tutorial qualifications which might be used on a sessional basis, by working for a distance-learning college or tutoring at a summer school.

Information   TASC Unit, Department of Education & Science, Elizabeth House, York Way, London SE1 7PH (Tel: 071 934 9000); City & Guilds of London Institute, 46 Britannia Street, London WC1X 9RG (Tel: 071 580 3050); Royal Society of Arts, 8 John Adam Street, London WC2N 6EZ (Tel: 071 930 5115).

WORK IN ENGINEERING AND SCIENCE

Two such vast work areas, ranging from metallurgy to biomedical electronics, need more than a few paragraphs in a returners' guide. If you have the maths and science background to be able to embark on any one of the technologies embraced under the general heading of 'science and engineering', then you'll need much more information. The *Careers Encyclopedia* (Cassell) is a useful starting point.

I suspect, though, that the average woman returner, while aware of efforts to widen girls' career horizons, and give them equal opportunities in science and engineering, probably lacks the technical knowledge to take advantage of the expansion in training for women in technology. If this applies to you, and if you like the idea of starting a second career in an engineering or scientific field, a one-week HILIGHT course, organized during the summer by the Engineering Industry Training Board could be your launch-pad. You need only to be over 21 and 'able to show you can succeed in higher education'. The free courses include conversations with women engineers, visiting an engineering company, learning about engineering courses and qualifications and sampling a HITECC conversion course – a free one-year course to bring you up to degree-entry standard in maths and physics. You're eligible for a local authority mandatory grant both for this course and if you subsequently decide to take up a degree place in a field like engineering, science, computing, building, manufacturing systems or teaching craft, design and technology.

Of course, you don't have to aim as high as a degree if you don't want to. Just as there are support-level jobs in fields like accountancy and law, so there are technician level jobs in areas like electronics, materials testing, computing, food technology and quality control. You can train for these through BTEC courses at local colleges. Colleges and local employers work closely together to devise the content of such courses and keep them up to date, so the range of BTEC courses in your local college prospectus is also a good guide to the likely demand for technicians in specific fields in your home area. One snag – you will find grants are only 'discretionary' for courses below BTEC Higher National level, so you might have to finance yourself unless you can find an employer prepared to give you day-release for a BTEC Certificate course. Ask the Jobcentre which firms to approach.

The UK suffers from a severe shortage of engineers and scientists, so if you get a qualification in any technological field and are prepared to use it in manufacturing or processing industries in your locality, you should have little difficulty getting a job.

Information Engineering Careers Information Service, 54 Clarendon Road, Watford WD1 1LB (Tel: 0923 38441).

WORK WITH FIGURES AND FINANCE

Accounting, banking, insurance, public finance

Every kind of activity, from running a supermarket to staffing an operating theatre, requires a sound financial basis and careful records of supplies used and time spent. If you have a gift for calculating and comparing, quantifying and evaluating, there could be a second career for you involving figures and finance.

These are also areas where studying by correspondence course has become well-established for examinations of all the accountancy bodies, building society and insurance institutes, as well as for local government and Civil Service promotion. This widespread home-study provision could help many a mature student who must earn while she learns (see Chapter 7).

Firms of accountants, banks, building societies and insurance companies which have all been accustomed to taking on teenagers from school or choosing graduates for management training may take some persuading to employ a 30- or 40-year-old beginner. Talk to your local Jobcentre about the attitudes of firms in your district. There may be some who are favourably disposed towards late-starters as a result of their experience of work with Employment Trainees (see Chapter 5).

In accountancy, an excellent reputation has been created by the support-level work of accounting technicians, whose qualification is recognized by all the professional bodies. Under 21s usually need four GCSEs to be accepted, but there are entry concessions for mature students.

In public service, eg, local government, district health authorities or tax or VAT offices, you may well find that mature entrants are welcomed and encouraged to study for qualifications that will improve their promotion prospects. In the Civil Service, there is no formal upper age limit for entry at administrative assistant level (with GCE or GCSEs), or administrative officer (with GCE or GCSEs, and sometimes A-levels). For executive officer work (with A-levels, HNC/D or degree), which may involve considerable responsibility or specialized training, the upper age limit is 50. Again, the Jobcentre is your best source of information about opportunities as vacancies are normally advertised locally.

Don't overlook the possibilities of work where you are concerned with quantities and costs rather than records and accounts. As examples, you might work in a hospital supplies department or train as a quantity surveying technician. Check the careers guides listed in the Appendix for details of these and other kinds of occupation concerned with quantitative work.

Information   **Accountancy**: Association of Accounting Technicians, 21 Jockey's Fields, London WC1R 4BN (Tel: 071 404 4961); Institute of Chartered Accountants of England and Wales, PO Box 433, Chartered Accountants' Hall, Moorgate Place, London EC2P 2BJ (Tel: 071 628 7060; see national phone directories for Scottish and Irish Institutes); Chartered Association of Certified Accountants, 29 Lincoln's Inn Fields, London WC2A 3EE (Tel: 071 242 6855); Chartered Institute of Management Accountants, 63 Portland Place, London W1M 4AB (Tel: 071 580 2311); Chartered Institute of Public Finance and Accountancy, 3 Robert Street, London WC2N 6BH (Tel: 071 930 3456). **Banking**: Banking Information Service, 10 Lombard Street, London EC3V 9AS (Tel: 071 626 8486). **Building societies**: Chartered Building Societies Institute, 19 Baldock Street, Ware SE12 9DH (Tel: 0920 5051). **Insurance**: Chartered Insurance Institute, The Hall, Aldermanbury, London EC2V 7HY (Tel: 071 606 3835). **Local government**: Local Government Training Board, Arndale Centre, Luton LU1 2TS (Tel: 05482 451166). **Civil Service**: Civil Service Commission, Alencon Link, Basingstoke RG21 1JB (Tel: 0256 29222).

WORK IN HEALTH CARE

Nursing
Of all occupations, this is the one that has given most thought to attracting mature students to make up the shortfall of school-leaver entrants, at the same time as reviewing, and experiment-

ing with, methods of training. The average upper age limit for entry to training is 45, with some schools taking people aged up to 50 and one or two welcoming those aged up to 55 (see *The Kogan Page Mature Student's Handbook*).

Nursing training is now concentrated on courses for Registered Nurse status, with a sharp reduction in the provision of courses for the support-level Enrolled Nurse qualification which is gradually being phased out. As well as the traditional three-year combination of practice and theory at hospital-based training schools, there are now college-based courses known as 'Project 2000' schemes. Hospital-based students are trained with pay; they are regarded as part of the care team and must share in the routine work as well as learning. College-based students get a training allowance; they attend hospitals and clinics to gain practical experience but are not seen as part of the workforce.

In several districts, there are now extended part-time Registered General Nurse training courses, held within school terms and hours, with school holidays off. A number are listed in *The Kogan Page Mature Student's Handbook*.

For both hospital-based and college-based Registration courses, candidates with either five O-levels/GCSEs including English, or the United Kingdom Central Council test of verbal reasoning, English and Maths, which is intended for mature students, are considered. Some training authorities also welcome mature students who have taken a Nursing Access course or a BTEC Health Sciences course (enquire locally).

A third way of qualifying is to take a combined nurse training and degree course. Here, again, the trainee nurse is paid a student grant rather than a salary, and is based at a university or polytechnic. These are usually four-year courses including clinical placements in hospital or the community lasting up to eight weeks. Though mature students are considered, competition for places is very keen and it is unlikely that candidates without A-levels would be considered. There are a few shortened courses for candidates with degrees in subjects other than nursing.

It is worth noting that there promises to be far greater scope for Registered Nurses to work outside hospitals as patients are discharged for 'care in the community'. In one speciality – work with mentally handicapped people – students of nursing and students of social work are already sharing some lectures in subjects where their future responsibilities may overlap.

Information   English National Board Careers Advisory Centre, 26 Margaret Street, London W1N 7LB (Tel: 071 388 3131); Welsh National Board, Cathays Park, Cardiff CF1 3AG (Tel: 0222 395535); Scottish National Board, 22 Queen Street, Edinburgh EH2 1JX (Tel: 031 226 7371); National Board for Northern Ireland, RAC House, 79 Chichester Street, Belfast BT1 4JE (Tel: 0232 246333).

Paramedical services

Among the professions which support and supplement medicine are Chiropody, Dietetics, Medical Laboratory Technology, Occupational Therapy, Orthoptics, Physiotherapy, Radiography and Speech Therapy. (A survey 'Attitudes to Mature Applicants for Training in Professions Supplementary to Medicine' quotes age limits, entry concessions and addresses of UK training centres. For a copy, send a cheque or postal order for £2.50, made out to Sheffield Education Authority, to the Sheffield Adult Guidance and Information Service, Sheffield Careers Service, AEU House, Furnival Gate, Sheffield S1 3S1.)

Some paramedical careers offer a choice between a three-year full-time non-graduate professional course, or a degree course which satisfies statutory requirements for registration. Dietetics and speech therapy, though, are all-graduate professions and though some training centres welcome people with alternatives to A-levels or Access courses, competition for places means they cannot always be as flexible as they would like in considering late-starters.

Upper age limits for entry to radiography and occupational therapy tend to be higher than for physiotherapy, and schools point out that this is a physically strenuous career. For chiropody, schools may require entrants to demonstrate manual dexterity. If you are free to travel anywhere to train, there is a chance of being accepted for one or more of the paramedical professions up to the age of about 50. Otherwise 40–45 is a usual upper age limit, sometimes lower for physiotherapy. The considerable scientific content of all the courses means that although generous entry concessions are usually offered to mature entrants, you will normally be encouraged to pass a science A-level or offer an OU science-based credit as preparation for training. As always, previous related experience, as a hospital 'aide' or voluntary worker, is an advantage and many training schools expect you to have observed work in the appropriate hospital department before applying for training.

Bursaries for non-graduate courses in occupational therapy, radiography and physiotherapy are given by the Department of Health, North Fylde Central Office, Norcross, Blackpool FY3 3TA. You can still be considered for a bursary if you have had a previous local education authority grant (for instance, for a degree course). For the other paramedical professions, it's a question of seeking local education authority finance: a mandatory grant if you have not previously had one, or perhaps a discretionary award if you have. Seek advice directly from your own LEA.

Information Society of Chiropodists, 8 Wimpole Street, London W1H 3PE (Tel: 071 580 3228); British Dietetic Association, 101 Daimler House, Paradise Circus, Queensay, Birmingham B1 2BJ (Tel: 021 643 5483); British Association of Occupational Therapists, 20 Rede Place, London W2 4TU (Tel: 071 229 9738); British Orthoptic Society, Tavistock House North, Tavistock Square, London WC1H 9HX (Tel: 071 273 5280); Chartered Society of Physiotherapy, 14 Bedford Row, London WC1R 4ED (Tel: 071 242 1941); The College of Radiographers, 15 Upper Wimpole Street, London W1M 8BN (Tel: 071 935 5726).

WORK IN HOTELS AND CATERING

Women who want to make second careers in hotel and catering work will find that, in most parts of the UK, employers are very willing to offer duty shifts that suit their home commitments, and are not particularly concerned about age. With a 24-hour service to provide, it is in any hotelier's interest to recruit local people who do not need accommodation or transport home after late shifts. Entry requirements are flexible – a pleasant manner and a genuine interest in the work are often the most welcome qualities.

From a modest start, helping in the kitchens or cleaning rooms and making beds, it's perfectly possible to work your way up the responsibility ladder by taking skills tests or evening classes. 'Caterbase' specific skill tests can be passed by assessment in the workplace and used as a foundation for City & Guilds courses. City & Guilds certificates plus experience can qualify the holder to embark on part-time study for HCIMA (Hotel, Catering & Institutional Management Association) professional exams.

If you choose catering rather than hotel work, you may train in schools or colleges, in industrial catering, in restaurants, with banqueting services, even in motorway catering facilities (contracts for the latter are often held by famous catering groups whose widespread activities mean you have extensive job possibilities in the long term). You may decide to specialize in some creative skill like patisserie, or develop an interest in a business area such as buying.

Many women who embark on careers in hotel or catering work eventually set up in business for themselves, running private catering services or sometimes purchasing a guest house to accommodate holidaymakers in summer and students in term-time. This may seem a distant prospect if you are at the stage of applying to the School Meals Service or trying for term-time work with Thistle Hotels (mentioned specially because they offer work which fits in with school holidays), but it does no harm to feel you are working towards a specific objective.

There are full-time City & Guilds, BTEC and degree courses in hotel and catering subjects, though in general, percentages of mature students on them are small. It is worth asking if Employment Training in hotel and catering work is available through your Jobcentre.

Information Hotel, Catering & Institutional Management Association, 191 Trinity Road, London SW17 7HN (Tel: 081 672 4251); Hotel & Catering Training Board, International House, High Street, Ealing W5 5DB (Tel: 081 579 2400).

MARKET RESEARCH, SELLING AND MARKETING

If you think that simply 'marketing' would have been a comprehensive enough title for this section, you're quite right and probably come from a marketing or management background. The reason I have started with market research and selling is that they are far easier for the mature entrant to penetrate than marketing itself. Companies commonly advertise for young graduates to embark on the complete marketing process as trainees, redistributing them to advertising, market research, home and international sales and customer service according to the abilities they develop. (A mature graduate who had demonstrated a flair for sales by, say, organizing and getting sponsors for a charity event at college might well be considered with the 22-year-olds for this kind of training.)

Marketing executives are most impressed by proven success, and in most parts of the country there are opportunities from time to time for mature women to work as market research interviewers. Conditions vary: you may have to be prepared to work at weekends or in the evenings, calling on people at home, and you may need your own transport. Good interviewers are likely to get more assignments or be promoted to a supervisory position – one woman I know ended up handling public relations for the market research company she initially joined as an interviewer.

Selling on behalf of a manufacturer or the provider of a service (such as transport or contract cleaning) is another field in which maturity is often regarded as an asset. By looking at 'situations vacant' advertisements, you will often find that manufacturers seek people aged 25–40 (sometimes older for private health insurance or pension plans where your own life experience is something you can draw on to convince others). Past work experience may have given you product knowledge: if you have been a teacher, you will be knowledgeable about educational materials, or if you have worked in a hospital, you can talk authoritatively about different types of disposable equipment.

Though marketing trainees have traditionally been recruited direct from university or polytechnic, it remains possible for late-starters who enter via market research or sales to be encouraged to move on into a company's marketing department – though good sales representatives may find they prefer the freedom of working (almost) independently!

Information Institute of Marketing, Moor Hall, Cookham, Maidenhead SL6 9QH (Tel: 062 85 24922); Market Research Society, 175 Oxford Street, London W1R 1TA (Tel: 071 439 2585); Institute of Sales & Marketing Management, Georgian House, George Street, Luton LU1 2RD (Tel: 0582 411130).

WORK IN OFFICE AND INFORMATION SERVICES

When new technology first appeared in offices, there were dire warnings about the job losses it would cause: secretaries would be replaced by word-processing equipment, telephonists by answering machines, filing clerks by computers. As we can readily see from the pages of situations vacant in the press and the office employment bureaux in every high street, the scenario is very different. With the advent of computers to store information, word-processors to edit and print it and fax machines to distribute text, and even diagrams, over the phone, secretaries are now office organizers, using the electronic technology for repetitive work and concentrating their efforts on management support work, like planning meetings, communicating with clients and devising mail shots.

But office technology has done more than just speed up the work of processing and distributing information. Since errors can be observed, corrected and double-checked before material is printed, secretaries no longer need to be super typists to succeed in office work. In the same way that calculators have opened up new career horizons for would-be scientists who were always held back by their lack of mathematical ability, word-processing equipment has simplified work with words. This means that more people can now use office skills as a starting point for a career in business.

How far you progress from your entry point with typing and word-processing skills is very much up to you, but it is fair to say that few businesses can operate at all without clerical and secretarial staff. For example, you are certainly more likely to get a foothold in television, publishing or international fund-raising if you possess office skills than with any other qualifications. Once on the inside, you are also first to hear of opportunities for training and promotion.

In many places, Jobcentres and further education colleges collaborate to provide practical and theoretical training in office technology and routines. 'Refresher' and 'Updating' courses are widely advertised, both at state and private colleges. (London Chamber of Commerce & Industry, Royal Society of Arts and Pitman qualifications are particularly highly regarded.)

Information London Chamber of Commerce & Industry, Marlowe House, 109 Station Road, Sidcup D15 7BJ (Tel: 081

302 0261); Royal Society of Arts, 8 John Adam Street, London WC2N 6EZ (Tel: 071 930 5115); Pitman Examinations Institute, Catteshall Manor, Godalming GU7 1UU (Tel: 048 68 5311).

WORK IN PERSONNEL, TRAINING AND CAREERS GUIDANCE

Many of the letters sent to me by readers ask about the possibility of late entry into these fields of work. Sometimes they come from people who have studied Psychology as an evening class choice or for an Open University degree, and who feel that work that involves the selection, welfare, motivation and development of people would make the most of their abilities. Sometimes women who worked as supervisors or management trainees before leaving to raise a family decide that they would like to return to the workplace having gained a better understanding of 'what makes young people tick', as one correspondent described it. And – certainly a compliment to the Careers Service – many a parent writes in to say that she's been impressed with the wide knowledge and effective advice of a careers officer who has guided her son or daughter, and can't think of a more worthwhile career to enter.

It is not absolutely necessary to have a degree to enter training for any of these three areas of work, but you will find that a majority of entrants are graduates – so you must offer some other qualification that is valuable and/or be prepared to start at a modest clerical level in a personnel, training or careers information office to gain useful experience.

The Institute of Personnel Management sets an excellent example by offering a Certificae in Personnel Practice examination which may be taken by people working in personnel departments, instead of A-levels, to satisfy its entrance requirements for student membership. Distance-learning facilities are available for the CPP.

Training instructors, officers and advisers need to have a sound and up-to-date knowledge base in the field where they hope to teach, so if you have had a gap in your employment history, you will almost certainly need to catch up on the latest methods before you can be seriously considered. Again, distance-learning packages have been created in most industries to help people update; there's also a *PICKUP Training Directory* which Jobcentres can access for you. When you find relevant employment, study for the Diploma of the Institute of Training and Development to improve your long-term prospects.

The publicly-funded Careers Service is open to a very wide range of potential entrants, from candidates with a degree or professional qualification to those over 25 with substantial industrial experience in an environment where they have dealt with a variety of people. Some local authorities will offer support-level jobs to would-be careers officers so that they can get an impression of the range of activities in a busy careers office, and will then sponsor their employees on the one-year full-time or two-year part-time training course. Mature candidates who are not able to get this kind of work experience, but who have had recent dealings with young people (perhaps as volunteer youth leaders) may be considered for the training course.

Information Institute of Personnel Management, 35 Camp Road, Wimbledon SW19 3VW (Tel: 081 949 9100); Institute of Training & Development, Marlow House, Institute Road, Marlow SL7 1BN (Tel: 0628 890123); Institute of Careers Officers, 27a Lower High Street, Stourbridge DY8 1TA (Tel: 038 43 86464).

WORK IN SOCIAL AND COMMUNITY SERVICE

Social work
No-one who reads a daily paper or watches television will be left in any doubt about the need for confidence, courage and a sense of responsibility in this profession. Most of us are now aware of the daily challenges faced by local authority social workers who may have to visit people living on estates where police patrol in pairs; take the responsibility for removing – or returning – a child whose parents have a dubious record of child care; or persuade a frail elderly client to move into supervised accommodation.

Add to this the need to assess and co-ordinate welfare provisions for people in need, understand medical, emotional and learning problems and be able to discuss solutions with other professionals, and you will appreciate why social work training authorities are constantly on the lookout for mature, responsible, tolerant people to train as social workers. The usual upper age limit for entry to training is 45, but some colleges will consider candidates aged up to 50.

Training is being reorganized and eventually all entrants will aim at a single qualification, the Diploma in Social Work. At present, the range of training options is very attractive to late entrants. For graduates, there are courses of one or two years in length, the shorter version being for people with 'relevant' degrees (those which have contained some practical social work). Others take a two-year (occasionally extended to three years) course leading to the Certificate of Qualification in Social Work. Those aged over 25 may be exempt from the normal minimum entry qualification of five O-levels/grades A–C GCSE passes.

For people working in residential social work, there is also a Certificate in Social Service qualification, allowing specialization in the care of particular groups, eg, adolescents, elderly people or residents with disabilities, and taken by day or block release. Again though, the plan is to replace the CSS. Although it is quite often possible to 'live in' if you choose, residential work does not invariably call for this, and it's quite common for residential social workers to take turns at sleeping-in duties on a rota system.

Many local authorities give discretionary grants to students taking the CQSW course. Some are sponsored by the Home Office for social work training for the Probation Service, and local authority employers will occasionally sponsor graduates on postgraduate social work courses, after they've had some in-service experience. Those who study by day or block release are normally paid during their time at college.

Youth work

If you get on well with teenagers and have skills you could share with them – in sport, drama, music or art, for example – you can test your suitability for making a career in youth work by helping on a voluntary basis at a youth club. This will also stand you in good stead when you apply for a place on one of the two-year (three years in Scotland) full-time, or occasional three-year part-time, courses leading to a Certificate in Youth and Community Work. The inclusion of the word 'Community' reflects an increasing trend for youth workers to involve themselves with all members of the community. Your work could include helping at English classes for immigrants, taking a turn at supervising an adventure playground or running a disco. As with social work, age limits are flexible, but people in their 20s and 30s may be preferred to those of 40 or 50 for a career that could be strenuous!

Information Central Council for the Education & Training of Social Workers, Derbyshire House, St Chad Street, London WC1H 8AD (Tel: 071 278 2455); Council for Education & Training in Youth and Community Work, Wellington House, Wellington Street, Leicester LE1 6HL (Tel: 0533 555666).

GRANTS
For degree and degree-equivalent courses (this includes Higher National Diploma courses and some professional courses) grants are mandatory (but means tested) from your home local education authority, ie, the one where you were educated. A free *Grants for students* guide is published by the Department of Education & Science, Elizabeth House, York Road, London SE1 8PH (Tel: 071 934 9000). For Scotland, write to the Scottish Education Department, Awards Branch, Haymarket House, Clifton Terrace, Edinburgh EH12 5DT (Tel: 031 556 8400).

If you have already had an LEA grant, or if you are applying for a course not designated for a mandatory grant, you can still apply for a discretionary award – again, your home local education authority is the one to consult. Discretionary awards may amount to as much as a mandatory grant, ie, payment of your tuition fees plus a living allowance, or amount simply to the payment of fees. The use of the word 'discretionary' means that the LEA can use its own discretion whether to give you an award or not. On some courses, a few students get awards and others have to pay their own way. Always ask – they can only say no, and they might say yes.

Department of Health bursaries are given to those studying for certain paramedical professions, including radiography, occupational therapy and physiotherapy. For details contact the Department of Health, North Fylde Central Office, Norcross, Blackpool FY3 3TA (Tel: 0253 63232).

MEMO TO EMPLOYERS AND TRAINING AUTHORITIES
Many returners are hesitant about even approaching the
organizers of training schemes which appear to have no age
limit. If, in fact, you are willing to retrain people who have taken
early retirement, it is worth saying so. You might try something
like, 'Most applicants will be aged between 25 and 45, but older
people with useful background experience will be carefully
considered'. Where your opportunities do not need previous
background experience, build on that strength with a comment
like, 'No experience necessary to join us as a Trainee Cook.
Day-release for mature people seeking new qualifications'.
Think about producing a careers leaflet aimed at returners,
getting across the demands of the job and inviting candidates to
contact you, using a tear-off application form.

CHAPTER 9

EARNING AT HOME

FITTING WORK INTO YOUR LIFE

Excuse me while I stir the split pea soup. Better organized journalists would probably have used the batch-cooking method weeks ago, and have their split pea soup frozen in tidy cubes, ready to re-heat in individual portions as required. On the other hand, as I pointed out to my hungry family some 20 minutes ago, given that I need to meet the delivery date for this book, and have to cope with requests from two magazines for regular copy and one magazine for a new feature, it's a wonder we're not all living on takeaways. (We probably would, if the takeaway was within walking distance.)

Also, of course, I must remember to ring back the two clients who left messages on my answering machine while I was taking the cat to the vet. One message was from a client who wants me to discover whether there is a national drift towards starting the summer school holiday in mid-July rather than late July – that will affect his schedules. The other was from the fax bureau I use, saying that they had been unable to fax my article to the magazine that was waiting for it, and had I, perchance, given them the phone number instead of the fax number?

Such conflicting demands on time and concentration are typical of working at home. Whether you write, cook, dress-make, word-process, conduct market research interviews or run a cattery, you can depend upon it that when you are doing your home work, your domestic affairs will intervene, and vice versa.

It may sound rather off-putting for me to point out that if it was so very profitable to work at home, no-one would pay vast sums to rent offices and factories, still less invest in high-tech equipment and staff to run it, but it's as well to know from the start that competing with established business is going to be hard work. It isn't just that you probably don't have the capital to invest in the latest equipment or an extensive advertising campaign (neither of these may be necessary if you have an original idea and think of ways to promote it energetically). Nor is it true that if you work from home, you're regarded as some sort of second-class citizen by potential employers with plate-glass showrooms and their own personnel officers. Present them with a unique, personalized service that doesn't exist in their own workforce and you're home and dry.

No, if there's going to be a problem it is that by working at home, you expect your daily routine to be more flexible and give you more freedom than you could expect if you went out to a job. It's hard to accept that the reverse is true. To combine the new demands of working at home with your regular chores needs a great deal of self-discipline and very careful assessment and allocation of the time you have available. Indeed, one of the very first things you should do before you even consider working at home is find out just how much time you can really spare to take on home work on a regular basis.

ARE YOU FREE?
Check on your available hours between the period 9 a.m. to 6 p.m., which will cover clients who themselves start at nine and those who start at ten and finish late. Only allow for evening or weekend work if the business you are setting up depends on it (for instance, in catering, there are always weekend surges). If you have a partner to consider, or children who will need or expect your attention after school, talk about your plans and, if your work is going to change the family lifestyle, make sure everyone understands and will at least give it a whirl.

Be realistic about how long it will take you to do each task concerned with your home employment – on the basis of here and now, not what might be possible if the business takes off and is such a success that you can buy time-saving equip-ment or pay someone to help at home or make deliveries for you. Be realistic, too, about the amount of time you've been spending on maintaining your home and coping with family commitments.

Returning to work, even work that you'll be doing at home,

implies that you have been fully occupied with domestic activities, and they're not going to go away once you start earning at home. There's always the temptation to believe that it will all jog along splendidly if you're there to unload the washing machine in a spare moment, or prepare the supper casserole during your lunch break. In fact, it can be tougher to establish an effective routine when you work at home than when you take a job outside the home.

For one thing, you yourself are at home all the time. Even your coffee cup and soup bowl add to the washing up, and you're there to answer the door to the meter reader or the charity collector. You're home for your friends to ring you up – or drop in for a chat. 'Are you busy?' they'll say, having seen you typing like wildfire as they peeped through the living room window, or stepping over the paper pattern you've laid out on the floor. Also they, and you, are there to see the dust you haven't had time to bother about, and the beds you put off making becuase you had to get on with your work. No-one would know about this if you were working in an office or a shop and not there to answer the door.

MAY I RING YOU BACK?
Still harping on the hazards, as an individual working at home, you have no-one to protect you from the telephone. There's no efficient secretary or receptionist to find out who's calling and why. Since every one of your clients will think you are totally absorbed in his or her work to the exclusion of everything else, they will cheerfully interrupt you to find out how the work is going, ask if you could machine another 50 teddy bears by Friday or suggest you fax a draft diagram to them to save time.

True, the telephone answering machine is a great invention, and yes, if you contrive to sound really concerned at missing calls and keen to call back soon, people will put real messages on it. However, unless you genuinely have to go out, or you are desperate for a couple of quiet hours in which to finish decorating 100 petits fours, you'll find it best to grit your teeth, put down what you were concentrating on and talk to your client. He or she may go in search of a more responsive service from a larger organization if there's any suspicion that an individual is too busy to answer enquiries.

It is true that if you work for yourself, you can in theory

decide whether you will sew all night to finish a vital costume for a child dancing in a festival that very weekend, or, contrariwise, that you will not accept any interviewing assignments during the school holidays.

In practice, although you can sneak the odd couple of days off with flu – it happens to people in outside jobs, too – and when you are starting, you may have the enthusiasm to work at night or all weekend on a rush job, it's necessary to establish a routine of work; a pattern that suits you, satisfies your customers or clients and lets you lead a reasonably balanced home life. It's not as easy as it sounds. You will be surprised how many clients deliberately choose to ring you up between 1 and 2 p.m. because it's the lunch-hour, and of course you'll be there because you work at home. Some home-based workers have a big breakfast, a mug of soup at midday and family tea with the children, to cope with this problem. And, while you may feel it's only reasonable to sit down and enjoy your favourite soap opera in the evening when you've been working non-stop all day, clients with urgent needs – especially those who are friends – will probably phone you just as it has started. (NB this may be a justifiable time to put on your answering machine if it's your favourite programme and a great treat, but remember to turn it off again afterwards.)

'How lovely', friends will say, 'not to have to go out to work on a cold wet morning, but to be able to earn in the comfort of your own home.' On cold, wet mornings that certainly can be counted as an advantage. On lovely sunny mornings, it's less appealing. A feature of paid work that you do at home is that you're always conscious of it being there, piling up, waiting for your attention. Many people find it very hard to tear themselves away from the thesis they are typing or the chair they are restoring and actually have some leisure time. When clients are pleased with you and praise you to the skies, work is even more addictive.

Women whose domestic efforts have been taken for granted for many years are often very susceptible to this and could end up letting themselves be swamped with orders from appreciative strangers! Alas, any client's enthusiasm quickly wanes if delivery is late, so learn to resist blandishments to take on just one more job when you are already fully committed. You can decline very regretfully and if the work you have been asked to do is something that both you and the customer would find useful to tackle at another time, offer to do this. Someone whose sofa has needed re-upholstering for a year is often not too bothered to know she has to wait a month for you to start, unless there's some pressing event, like a family wedding, in view.

BUILDING A REPUTATION
I've so far assumed that you do have a good business idea and that you've presented it well so that you are in the happy position of having plenty of work. As everyone knows, it's not that simple, and the world is not crying out for women to type envelopes at home or become outworkers for factories – the two home employment ideas most often mentioned by women who write to magazine careers advisers for advice on finding customers. In practice, they are usually the least likely work sources, since in offices word-processing equipment now deals swiftly with envelope addressing, and in factories computer-controlled machinery deals with most routine assembly tasks. Other assembly work may need special conditions, eg, a sterile atmosphere, temperature-controlled environment, protective clothing, so cannot be done at home.

You can get ideas for a home business by reading how other people have done it. Booklets like *Working in Self Employment* (Careers & Occupational Information Centre) and guides like *Occupation – Self-Employed* (Wildwood House) include interesting case histories, but the fundamental need in every case is to discover what is required in *your* area and how you can provide it. For example, maybe you're a dressmaker. You may not be able to compete with chain stores on cost, but if, by liaising with local disability help groups or old people's day centres, you discover there's a demand for a dressmaker who will call on housebound clients with pattern books, measure them for the design of their choice and then go away and make up the garments, you could have the beginnings of a service that users will recommend to other potential clients.

Perhaps you're an accomplished linguist? Take time to update your skills with a course at the nearest polytechnic or university, and then consider how best to market yourself as a home worker to local employers. 1992 will create opportunities to trade all over the EEC. Large firms may already employ language specialists to promote their products or services, but what about the smaller firms? Is there a potential home business in offering to translate their sales literature into French, German, Italian, Dutch – or whichever community language you speak? Test the market by preparing a mail shot that demonstrates how well you can translate excerpts from different firms' existing leaflets and brochures. Be ready for a response that asks about the time you'd take to do a certain number of words; whether such material will be supplied in typewritten form or on disc; what your charges might be for something much more extensive, like a technical handbook. Work out costs per 1,000 words.

MISSING LINKS

Many a small business has started because someone has observed a gap in the market. Probably the most obvious example, which has also been well-publicized on TV, is that of the sandwich-maker who recognizes there's nowhere for workers to eat on the local industrial estate. Flower-sellers who set up business in lay-bys and second-hand booksellers who sell by mail order are other good examples.

But are there different needs or shortages in your own area? Watch the 'situations vacant' columns in the local paper and spot the advertiser who regularly appeals for secretarial staff. He or she could be highly susceptible to a home typing service based on the regular collection of audiotapes of work and their next-day delivery. Are local returners writing to the paper about the difficulty of finding supervised tea-and-homework sessions for over-tens? That could be the start of a regular care service for you. With friends who could share the cost of a hall with catering facilities, it might well be extended into a holiday play-care service, too.

Among the self-employed who have come knocking on my door in the last year are the man with an aerial view of my house which he thought I might like to buy, the designer of individual house nameplates and several people who wanted to resurface my drive. Meanwhile, by direct mailshot I've been invited to have my carpets cleaned *in situ*, to visit a sale of cut-price suede and leather goods and to attend an open day at a local alternative medicine centre. If you want to alert people to what you are offering, leaflets through doors can be a budget-wise investment (especially if you deliver them yourself).

FREE PUBLICITY

Local newspapers, radio stations and clubs are always in the market for news about new enterprises, and, more particularly, about the people setting them up. The newspapers and commercial radio stations often hope they'll get some advertising as a result of interviewing you or using your press release.

If you yourself are convinced of the merits of your home-earning project, it won't take you long to draft a press release about it – try it on your family and friends (always the most severe critics) before you send it out and remember to stay close to the phone for the next week or so, so that you don't miss any opportunity for a follow-up interview. Radio stations may ask you to come along and justify the need for a herbalist or 'keyboard skills for men' teacher in your area. Local clubs will often be happy to pay your expenses if you'll go along and talk about your special subject to their members. It's all valuable publicity and, once again, you should stay close to the phone for several days afterwards to pick up new clients who result from these efforts on your part.

KEEPING TRACK

As well as doing the actual job you have created for yourself, whether it's looking after someone else's cat or supplying window box flowers to local offices, you will have to allow time for basic business housekeeping. Making out record cards for clients, sending out quotations, re-ordering routine stationery, completing tax returns and checking on responses to advertisements or mail shots will be regular responsibilities. You should make a regular time for them. Friday afternoon would be quite a good choice – in most larger businesses, it's when the pace of work slackens and anything not really urgent is held over until Monday (of course if you're working in a field like tourism or catering where work peaks at the weekend, Monday afternoon could be a better time).

KEEPING GOING

Even if you work out a realistic timetable that takes into account your family lifestyle and routine, contriving to run a home and earn from home can be rather a lonely business. It's easier if you can interest your partner/relative/children in what you are doing so that they can share your joys and sorrows, but to be honest, if you are going to succeed in self-employment, you need to be self-reliant. You can hope for support and praise, but nobody except you will realize how much effort has to be put into thinking up an effective way of earning at home, publicizing it, launching it and developing it just enough – but not so much that you get overloaded with work and go under. Beware of expecting other people to be as interested and proud of your efforts as you are yourself – mostly, they don't appreciate what it takes to set up a business of your own.

Rather than hoping for praise from everyone around you, set your own targets so that you can pat yourself on the back or give a deep sigh of relief when you meet each one. For example, let's say you run a party buffet service or dressmake to order. You could set aside a time to work out a realistic scale of charges which you can send to enquirers or incorporate in an advertisement. That's a good task to have completed. Or you may specialize in wedding photography and need to phone round all the local churches to see if they have a magazine in which you could take advertising space for your service. That, too, is a valuable project – you can congratulate yourself when you've done it.

A useful tool is one of those splendid wall calendars with sticky symbols to use for visits, delivery dates, advertisements, and so on. In the early stages, however, you can get by with sheets of lined foolscap, one for each month, with a line for each day and different coloured pens for different tasks.

A MATTER OF ADJUSTMENT

If you once worked for an established organization, it will come as a shock to you to discover how much it costs to run a business. You probably took it for granted that there would always be stationery and typing ribbons in the cupboard, that you could use the phone whenever you wanted to call up a customer or a supplier, and that clients sent in requests for information as a result of reading your company's advertisement. Even the cleaning and heating of your workplace was probably something you took for granted, to say nothing of all the equipment supplied by the firm.

When you work from home, you are your own Supplies Manager, Finance Manager, Sales Manager and Production Manager. Unless you start off with a large injection of capital

– or perhaps even more if you start off that way – you will need to research the most cost-effective way of providing the service you have in mind or the products you want to make. You'll also have to find customers (and keep finding them, if you want to prosper) and you will have to allow for packing, postage or other delivery costs.

SMALL BUSINESS COURSES

These courses outline all the responsibilities for you and show you effective ways of dealing with them. It's an investment in your future to spend some time and money studying, for instance, the different ways of marketing a product or service; how to keep records of expenses and income that will satisfy the Inland Revenue and whether there are any laws concerning the sort of work you want to do at home that you should bear in mind.

Ask your local Jobcentre what is provided under the national Employment Training scheme in the way of Enterprise Training. This can range from classes in book-keeping and marketing, free to people considering self-employment, to occupational training if you need to acquire certain skills for your personal project, and advice on how to present a business proposal to a bank manager. (NB Under certain conditions, unemployed people may apply for the Government's Enterprise Allowance of £40 a week for 52 weeks to help them establish their business, but they must apply before starting the business – get all the details from the Jobcentre at an early stage of your planning.)

There are many sources of help and advice for the would-be entrepreneur, including the 'Business Books' section in your local public library. There you will find titles like Godfrey Golzen's *Going Freelance* (Kogan Page) or Christine Brady's *The Home Earner* (Transworld). Depending on the kind of business you want to run, my own *Running Your Office* (BBC Books) may be helpful. Check carefully through the selection of titles on display, and if you want to know if anyone's written a book about starting a guest house or setting up as an industrial photographer, ask the librarian for help.

If you have a professional qualification that you want to use in self-employment, go to your own professional institute for advice. If you have experience in a particular trade – groceries, say, or bookselling – check up with the employers' federation to see if any specific business literature has been produced, and to find out which trade magazines to read.

See the list of useful addresses in *Working in Self-Employment* (COIC) mentioned earlier. They range from the Rural Development Commission to the British Franchise Association and from Women in Enterprise to the Co-operative Development Agency. The most it will cost you to find out about their activities and whether they are relevant to your home earnings plan is time, stationery and a stamp – perhaps two stamps, if you enclose one for a rapid reply. You might discover you are eligible for a grant, loan or a place on a course that will greatly improve your chances of success.

Some people are natural entrepreneurs, some choose to learn small business skills and some are forced into self-employment. The last-named reason is not such a bad one as you might think. It means that you have to succeed, learning as you go along, adapting your ideas to suit the market and refusing to be beaten even when business is hard to find.

As a learning experience, some people feel that all would-be employees should first discover what is involved in making an enterprise pay its way. If your own efforts to learn at home do no more than this, you will be a much more useful employee if you eventually end up being employed by someone else. But with a reasonable amount of luck and a great deal of market research, careful costing and determined promotion, you could be the one to be offering employment in the long term. Remember, every business once started simply as an idea, which was turned into a profitable project.

MEMO TO EMPLOYERS

You have nothing to lose by considering any business or production service proposed to you by a home-based worker, provided, of course, that she offers a skill you may need at a cost that seems reasonable. Even if you are fully staffed when a mail shot or phone call from a would-be home worker comes in, remember that such a service could be worth calling on in an emergency – when you get a rush order, for example, or if flu descends on your staff. If the skills offered are never needed by your business, it's kind to say so, rather than just ignore the approach, and even kinder to send the leaflet, or refer the caller, to a business which might need such a service.

You may be the kind of employer who would be very glad to use the skills and experience of the home worker concerned if only she was free to work on your premises. Again, you lose nothing by making the offer and perhaps sending details of any employee facility you offer (like a crèche) that might make it possible for someone to consider working outside the home. Someone unable to take up an outside job because of family commitments at present may keep details of your company on file, and if their home business is not everything they hoped for, consider the possibility of taking up outside work. If you responded pleasantly to their approach, they are most likely to apply first to you for a job.

If you do decide to give an outside employee a try, be very clear about the service you expect – supply a worksheet with exact dimensions and methods if it is a case of making a product, or give written instructions if you are commissioning a translation, an article or a market research survey. Specify quantities or materials where this is appropriate or, with a task like typing a manuscript, give an example of the style to be followed. Always quote a delivery date and price in your commissioning letter. It is sensible to give yourself some leeway by setting the delivery date a few days ahead of actual need: just like the staff who work on your premises, outside workers can be struck down by flu or held up by children's illnesses and you wouldn't want to lose either your company's goodwill or a potentially useful outworker by having an inflexible policy on delivery times.

Explain your payments system to people working for themselves. It may seem reasonable to you that you normally pay at the end of the month following delivery, but this may be hopelessly uneconomic for someone without capital to live on (unless she has arranged overdraft facilities with a bank on the basis of your written explanation of your payment methods). The small business you help at the start is likely to be a loyal contributor to your enterprise from that moment on, and likely to repay your consideration by making great efforts to help you over any problems you encounter with rush orders or staff absences.

CHAPTER 10

DUAL-CAREER PLANNING

'But I'm not planning to have a career, I'm only returning to work part-time.' Perhaps you think you can skip this chapter, because you're not dynamic, thrusting and ambitious – just a Mum looking for an interesting part-time job that will help stretch the family budget.

Yet, even if this is true, the fact that you're going back to work is something that will affect your partner and children, or a dependent relative if that is one of your responsibilities. The ideas and tips in this chapter could be as useful for you as for the returner re-starting in full-time work, or retraining for a completely new career.

Jobs have a way of developing people. The ward clerk, in touch with patients and nurses all day long, can discover that she has leanings towards nursing, and that, when the children are older, she's going to take advantage of her hospital's welcome for mature students. Indeed, if the nursing school should introduce part-time training, she could begin almost at once. Careers can be thrust upon people. Often, supervisory work with young staff shows that a particular individual has a real flair for getting skills across. Training skills are greatly in demand in today's changing world and people who are not only unafraid of new technology themselves but also good at persuading other people to see its advantages, won't remain users but turn into trainers.

Often, a woman returning to work mainly for interest and to expand the family's financial horizons discovers that she's grown out of the job she did before having a family. She may not have intended to have a second career, but employers are quick to notice talent and make use of it. All of a sudden those three days a week working in the estate agent's showroom are extended by a Sunday afternoon demonstrating the show house and encouragement from the firm to take estate agency training and exams.

READY FOR ANYTHING?

Even if you agree that your return to work is just an experiment, to see how well it suits you and your family, it's essential to agree the priorities in your changed situation, particularly since it may go on changing and developing if you settle well into your new lifestyle. There are major and minor changes to be made in the way you organize your life and it pays to start introducing them before you step back into the workplace, wherever possible.

CHILD CARE

This demands the most careful research and experiment. Whether you are returning to a very highly-paid job that enables you to employ a live-in nanny, or looking for a registered child-minder for mornings only to enable you to ease yourself back into paid work, you need to satisfy yourself that the person caring for your child does it in a way you respect. You'll never find anyone who brings up children quite as you do, but you won't settle happily in any job or course if you are uneasy about the way your child is being looked after, or if the child is clearly unsettled and unhappy at your absence.

For an outline of the variety of child care available for under fives, read *Pre-school Choices* (Longman), which not only describes the differences between playgroups, nurseries, crèches etc, and outlines the regulations each must satisfy, but also points out examples of good practice that you can look for when investigating local facilities. There's advice on choosing a child-minder and on the sort of activities you can hope to see going on at a playgroup or nursery school.

When interviewing a nanny, ask questions about the kind of routine the nanny has been taught to use. Some mothers successfully share a nanny, and employing a nanny who has a small child of her own can also be very successful. The best arrangement I was ever lucky enough to make was with a friend who was a nurse in a children's hospital – she cared for her son and my son in my house. The children had the benefit of each other's company; my child had his familiar surroundings and the other child had his mother's care all day. It lasted until they were both old enough to go to nursery school.

Talking of nursery schools, it is now a commonplace for children to be invited to visit the nursery school that they will be attending, with their mothers, just to get an idea of what is going on before they actually join. They're shown where children hang up their coats, where the lavatories and wash-basins are, how children sit around and play with paints, and so on, so that the place is not completely unfamiliar when they start. Such a 'rehearsal' could be just as valuable with other kinds of care. If you are going to employ a nanny or send your child to a minder, you could start these activities before you return to work. It will be easier for both of you if the child-minding arrangement is up and running before you plunge back into employment. You'll find it a lot easier to re-adjust to working life if you know that your child is comfortably established in a caring situation that you have organized and that you know works well.

The need for child care does not stop at five years old when children start school, and it's this aspect that prevents so many women from returning to work. Employers like Boots and Thistle Hotels who offer term-time only contracts clearly appreciate the problem of the school holidays where parents who don't have Granny conveniently nearby to care for the children find themselves hunting for carers. They are a very small minority, though, and most employers find it difficult to give mothers time off without pay during school holiday periods.

Job-sharing can be a way of solving the problem. Just as two mothers can share a nanny, two mothers can share a job, looking after each other's child on their 'days off'. It is a policy you have to sell to employers, and you need to find your sharer, as well-qualified as you and perhaps with some attribute you don't possess so that in letting two people share one job, the employer gets the benefit of extra skills. Point out, too, that if one of the sharers (or sharers' children) is unwell, the other can often fill in during her absence, so that the work continues.

You can also contact local colleges which train nursery nurses or teachers to ask if any student is interested in babysitting –

and perhaps vacation work as a child-minder. Again, and as always, whenever you can experiment with child care, it's best to do so – if by some unlucky chance your child doesn't take to the babysitter, you can look elsewhere.

The holidays that present the greatest headache are the summer six or seven weeks, and if you have a husband or partner it is worth getting together to see if by pooling your holiday resources, you can't arrange to cover this period somehow. Many companies allow staff to have 'grace days' – an allowance of days off for dental appointments, moving house and similar family events – or will let people build up overtime for work done outside compulsory flexitime hours to make up days off. Your own days off allowance may not amount to much, but together you may be able to account for a fortnight or so. If you then take a fortnight's formal holiday, you have only to look for child care for two or three weeks. Many local authorities run play schemes for under-12s where it can be easier to book a place for part of the time than to occupy the whole summer holiday, or to afford a stay at a children's holiday centre. Numerous organizations run these, providing a range of varied entertainments from football to computing and drama to crafts. Ideally you should see a centre in action before you send your child off, but if that's not possible, ask if you can be put in touch with a parent who has had experience of the holiday centre and talk to her and her child about the place, so that you can judge whether it would suit your own child.

Under-tens are probably better off staying with a relative, a neighbour or in their own home, in the care of a student. You may have to offer generous pay to tempt a student during the summer break, but they don't all work relentlessly for the full vacation, and often enough, someone who hopes to holiday abroad will be glad to earn the money to pay for it by looking after a school-child for two or three weeks.

COPING WITH EMERGENCIES
Where child care is concerned, it's important to work out contingency plans in case something goes amiss. No-one likes to look on the black side, but just suppose your nine-year-old has to have his appendix out – you won't want to sit at home afterwards wrangling about who will ask for time off from work to mind him during the convalescent period. Less dramatically,

what's your contingency plan if Mrs Jones, who always picks up the children from school and takes them to her house for tea and play till you get home at six o'clock, suddenly has to devote the time to looking after her elderly mother? If you've found time to participate in parent-teacher activities as well as running a home and going to work, you can probably think of several mothers with children at the school who might help out in an emergency. Make sure you have as many telephone numbers as possible of people you might call on when you need to.

COPING WITH CHANGE

If you have decided to return to work, you may well be looking forward to the change from a personal point of view. Even if the job you are starting out in is not particularly exciting and you're only doing it because you need the money, then at least having the extra cash will motivate you to put up with the effort and re-adjustments you will probably have to make.

Those around you may be less enthusiastic about the prospect. Your husband or partner may recognize the need for you to work but also wish very much that you could continue in your home-based role (particularly if you're good at it!). Children and/or elderly dependents will almost certainly be apprehensive at what seems to be a huge change in their established lifestyle. A very small child may not realize that you are not safely at home all day, awaiting his or her return from nursery, but an older child will know that you're working in the bank or at the hotel, and are inaccessible save for the direst emergency. Only the most bouncily confident will be unaffected. With others, you can expect insecurity to be expressed in ways that range from, 'I don't want any breakfast. I have a tummyache' to 'I don't see why I should have to drag round the supermarket with you. Other people's mothers do the shopping while they're at school'.

Elderly relatives, regretfully left for two or three hours because you need the money to help maintain them, may think up tasks to delay you: their hot water bottle is cold; they've lost the remote control for the TV or the piece of paper on which you've written your phone number – you simply can't go yet.

If you think ahead, then to a very great extent you can avert many of these reactions. Children and old people, like everyone else, are more likely to respond to the carrot than the stick. They need convincing of the advantages of your return to work, so if, for instance, you begin by saying, 'Let's plan what we're going to have for supper this week. Now I'm earning some extra money, we can afford to have more of our favourite meals. What shall be buy?' (or with a child, 'Let's go and choose').

There's often some longed-for activity that it's been hard or impossible to afford until more money is brought into the house. It's reasonable to say, 'I know you want ballet lessons and if this job I'm doing works out, we should be able to afford them. Let's see how we all manage for a couple of weeks and then, if everything is going well, we'll arrange for you to start at the dancing school.'

The older the person you are dealing with, the more praise and reassurance they will need. Husbands as well as elderly dependent relatives need to be told, 'I'd never be able to manage this job if it wasn't for you'. (For elderly relatives: 'It's such a help to know you are here to answer the phone; welcome the children home from school; listen to my problems when I've had a bad day.') It should go without saying that you also need to be ready to listen to other people's problems as required – co-operation is a two-way business.

As well as thinking of – and acting on – ideas that show those around you how much everyone has to gain from your return to work, you need to deal with insecurities. For school-age children, being able to use the telephone can be a valuable accomplishment. Give them a phone card and coins so that they can get in touch with you if what they deem an emergency occurs.

Obviously, you must impress upon them that just as their teacher wouldn't be very pleased if you walked in in the middle of a lesson, so your boss won't be too pleased if you ring up Mum at work, unless it's really important. In practice, most children, even teenagers, are a little scared of ringing unknown people anyway, so they're not very likely to ask your switch-board to find you unless it is an emergency. The phonecard in the top pocket is as much a comfort blanket as anything else.

If you are inaccessible – perhaps you are a sales representative and can't be sure where you can be contacted at any given time of day – then a child, teenager or elderly dependent relative needs to have access to someone else who can cope in an emergency. A husband or partner may be the obvious choice, but a relative or a neighbour could be just as suitable.

For an elderly person, the name and phone number of the doctor and, if they so choose, a vicar or priest, should be clearly written in block capitals on white paper and stuck with transparent adhesive tape to the bed-table or coffee table near to the phone. Pieces of loose paper can drop on to the floor where they can't be reached. Sudden fears or the onset of an illness can make it difficult to focus on handwriting: if the vital numbers are in bold black capitals and actually stuck to the surface on which the phone rests, it's more likely that the elderly person will be able to use them when really necessary.

Again with elderly people, it will help if you can set up some pleasant event that will occur as a result of your absence. I once interviewed a very frail but just mobile lady of 96 whose home help always laid ready a trolley with biscuits or cake and tea in flasks for her afternoon visitors. Trusted friends like the vicar and the library lady knew where to find a key to let themselves in; strangers like me had to identify themselves before the door was opened on a chain. Some adaptation of this sort of scheme could mean that a housebound person gets more company when you are at work than when you were at home all day.

HUSBANDS AND PARTNERS

These people need as much preparation for your return to work as do children and grannies or grandads, probably more so – unless they are either desperate for your earnings because the mortgage company is threatening to foreclose, or strongly feminist in their views (in which case you'd feel guilty if you enjoyed staying at home). Even the enthusiasts may waver in the early days of coping with the reality of a dual-career lifestyle.

Most men would fall into the 'don't know' category if asked whether they approved of women working if the household didn't need the money, or would say 'it all depends'. Certainly, if you're a naturally good cook and housekeeper, anyone who has luxuriated in your care is going to feel rather as if the rug has been pulled from under him when you trip off to work again.

Demonstrating that your provision for dependents is well thought out and effective is bound to be reassuring, but the future for both of you is going to involve a completely new way of living, one in which you'll both almost certainly have to work harder or more effectively, and which is going to provide more cash for you to share, or possibly to save towards some special project.

If you are returning to work purely for pleasure and satisfaction, and your earnings are not needed for everyday expenses, your career plans may be more eagerly listened to if some of your earnings, at least, will be used for the general good: a super holiday, central heating, or perhaps paying for that distance-learning MBA that your husband couldn't otherwise justify.

Arguments about where the money goes, whether it's worth your while to work when you pay out so much for child care or whether you can justify taking a three-year retraining course for that career you've always wanted to enter, are less likely to occur if the basic comforts of the home remain the same. It is hard to be resentful when, if you are first in at night, you find a tray laid for a quick snack, a tidy living room and a heater just waiting to be lit. If on the other hand, the first person home is met with a sinkful of dirty dishes, the ashes of last night's fire and the knowledge that any minute now, a child will arrive demanding a big tea because school dinner was horrible, it's harder to justify the dual-career family arrangement.

It is better to start off by sitting down and considering how you can keep things running smoothly when much of your time will be spent at work. Different ways of doing things, and in the long run extra equipment, may be necessary. But to begin with, you and your partner need to agree on the priorities – what it is that makes home 'homelike' and how you can contrive to provide those essentials in the new circumstances.

It's no good pretending that home will be quite the same when two people ignore it all day in favour of an outside job. What you see when you leave at 8 a.m. is what you're going to get when you return at 6 p.m., so you will have to decide whether you'll change your early morning routine or your early evening expectations!

We all develop our own systems. I used to skip my breakfast in order to feed husband and children (not always luxuriously, and remembering how guilty I used to feel about some of my scrappy efforts, it's maddening to learn now that my children's happiest memories include 'eating fishpaste sandwiches in Dad's car on days when we'd be late for school'). Having missed breakfast and with a train journey to get to my work, I'd have coffee and rolls in the station buffet on arrival, or if I, too, was running late, hold the hunger till coffee time when I'd have a bun from the canteen.

Your routine could involve cooking porridge overnight in a slow cooker, or using a microwave to make instant scrambled egg, or giving the family cornflakes plus a substantial mid-morning snack. And if you don't have a dishwasher (rarely affordable when you need it most) it's less horrific to return to the breakfast dishes soaking in the bowl, or preferably rinsed off and dried off during the day in a draining rack, than to find them caked with hours-old cereal or bacon fat when you return from work.

One reasonably tidy downstairs room is essential, not just because of callers who will gossip about the way you live, but because you deserve somewhere pleasant to relax after your work.

Re-arrange your furniture so that at the end of the day, you can gather up toys, newspapers and other rubble and deposit it in a large cardboard box to hide behind the sofa. Open the windows to give the room a good airing while you're doing this, shake up the cushions, if any, and be ruthless about throwing out dying flowers. I don't suggest you vaccum at 10 p.m. but you might manage a quick whisk round before work if you're terribly efficient, and if not, it's much less discouraging to have to face vacuuming a clear floor space when you get in from work than to have to begin by picking up a lot of 'litter'.

If your family is anything like mine, you will find it is a constant battle to keep the tops of kitchen units clear to work on, and that as the week wears on there is a gradual build up of coffee jars, teabags, opened sliced loaves, paper tissue packets, tin-openers, etc. Nagging is ineffective and you may have to learn to live with it. If 'what people think' worries you (it does me), then leaving space at the front of your kitchen cupboards so that you can hastily stuff these items out of sight in a matter of moments has a certain amount going for it.

The one room you will never be forgiven for leaving in a scruffy condition is the bathroom and/or loo. 'It's not fair,' you may justifiably complain to yourself, as you dash round with cleaning powder and disinfectant, 'why doesn't someone else do this?' Unless you also service the car, change the lightbulbs and get the black bags ready for dustbin day, you're unlikely to be able to get Someone Else to share toilet duty, though it can help to send children away on holidays with the Scouts or Guides where they discover that in an ideal world everyone shares chores on a rota, or at least is supposed to do so.

Foodwise, if you can knit or sew while you watch TV, you can also peel potatoes and prepare sprouts on a tray on your lap. It shouldn't spoil your enjoyment of the programmes and it is a great timesaver.

As well as finding easier ways to do jobs like these, think about having emergency supplies of the things you really must not run out of. Bread mix in a packet will save you on the day you forget to buy bread and there must be sandwiches for school lunch tomorrow. Dogs will eat meatballs and cats usually adore pilchards in tomato sauce on the day you forget the petfood. Most animals will eat scrambled eggs, too, when you can't stand those appealing eyes, mews and whines any longer.

In the days when I really needed it, I didn't have a freezer, so I developed a repertoire of recipes that could be hastily concocted from tins and packets. Mince with added onion, stock and dumplings (from a mix) remains a favourite. Rice with grilled chopped luncheonmeat, chopped tinned kidney, a couple of tablespoons of baked beans for colour and a sauce made of the kidney liquor, water, stock and cornflour started out as an emergency concoction and is now remembered with affection when I dish up posher risotto from the freezer.

Does all this make you shudder? In that case you are probably a splendidly creative cook already and need no tips from the likes of me. Many healthier meals can also be prepared in advance, and you can always revert to your slowly and carefully prepared five-course blow-out at the weekends or on special occasions.

WORKING FOR A BETTER LIFESTYLE
Possibly, if you are already feeling a bit doubtful about returning to work at this stage of your life, my well-meant anecdotes are discouraging you. If so, remember that when you are earning more, you can afford more of the timesavers that make life pleasant. Your target may be a washer-dryer, freezer, automatic cooker, microwave – or three hours a week from a genuinely domesticated helper.

You may feel that your life consists of shopping for meals that you cook for people who consume then leave you to wash up. If so, earning more money could mean more meals out, more picnics in summer, more visits to friends, more purposeful cooking, eg, for entertaining. It may mean hotel holidays instead of self-catering chalets; a second car that means you can drive yourself to the supermarket for late-night shopping and wander peacefully up and down the aisles without people tugging at your coat and saying, 'Haven't you finished yet?' or 'Why can't I have sugar crispies instead of rotten old muesli?'

For everyone in the family, your return to work will be a time of adjustment, and that includes you. In the early days, when there always seems to be something left undone, don't let yourself be distracted by what you haven't accomplished. Instead, when you go to bed at night, think about the new skills you've learned, the targets you're aiming at, the home-making chores you are teaching your children.

CHAPTER 11

BUILDING ON YOUR STRENGTHS

NEW HORIZONS

When you first return to work, you'll probably be mainly concerned with keeping things ticking over satisfactorily at home while you find your feet in your new environment. But once you settle into a routine and feel in control of your life, it would be surprising if you didn't want to look around and see if there are ways of improving your circumstances. It's human nature to seek approval and look for proof that your efforts are appreciated.

Not everyone wants to move upwards and onwards; sometimes it's a sideways move into a different kind of work or a widening of responsibilities that gives job satisfaction. The need to progress and develop, though, is something most of us are aware of as we go through life.

For the woman returner, half the battle is to feel justified in seeking advancement. It's perhaps hardly surprising after generations of women have been expected to get their job satisfaction from rocking the cradle and washing the socks that the present generation needs persuading that they're entitled to enjoy working outside the home.

Once you've proved to yourself that you can manage a home and a job, it's natural to look towards the next achievement.

Good employers trigger ambition by offering in-service training courses to eligible employees. Once you've been at work for three or six months, say, you could become eligible for a two-day course in a word-processing system that's new to you, or a seminar on health and safety at work.

Some women can feel rather guilty when they leave their

regular work to take a training course, even if it's provided by the employer and they're paid as usual. If you're bothered by such feelings, remind yourself that more often than not, the people whose jobs are made redundant are those who have ignored opportunities to update and learn new skills, and that it's the employer's responsibility to give you this extra training.

Don't, for goodness sake, do what I did once and think that because you are offered extra training, it's a criticism of the way you are already working. This happened to me when I was at the BBC, presenting a regular item as part of a magazine programme. I was very taken aback when I was offered a place on a 'presentation' course. What could I have been doing wrong? Why had nobody told me I was making mistakes? Regrettably, hard on the heels of those thoughts came one along the lines of, 'Well, if I'm not good enough for them as I am . . .' and I voiced these views to the management, though in a less aggressive way.

Of course, I was told that the presentation course was a compliment; that I'd done so well without training, they wanted to see how far I could go once I'd been taught professional skills; that everyone's performance could be improved and that had I chosen to go on the course, I might have been offered more opportunities to present programmes instead of the single item that I fronted each week. However, since I didn't feel enthusiastic, of course I needn't attend the training sessions.

Yes, you've guessed. I didn't get offered any new opportunities to present programmes, and funnily enough, having turned down the offer of extra training, I began to pick holes in my own broadcasting techniques when I listened to recordings. Moral: 'Why me?' is a much wiser response than 'What, me?' if you are offered a place on a training course or seminar.

REVEALING POTENTIAL
Being invited to upgrade your skills or knowledge is a positive indication that you are being considered for other things – not necessarily more advanced work, but possibly different responsibilities. You lose nothing by trying your hand at something new (if it only teaches you that you are well-placed where you are, that's worth knowing) and you add to your work record the fact that you have responded to offers of extra training. Rejecting training, as you'll have seen from my own experience,

is likely to saddle you with a reputation for being big-headed or unco-operative or both!

It can be constructive to ask 'Why me?' particularly if you've been picked out of a group of people doing similar work. The answer could be as unexciting as, 'Well, we always offer this course to anyone once they've been with us for six months'. However, it might be, 'We're thinking of buying a text editing system and we feel you could be the right person to run it', or 'We've noticed that you get on very well with the YTS trainees, and we feel that given some extra training, you could be a good supervisor for them'.

If you've shown potential above and beyond the range of your basic responsibilities, you may even be invited to move out of your speciality and join the trainee management stream of employees. When this happens, as it often does, to someone who has returned to work expecting to use technical or scientific qualifications, it can be quite traumatic. Do you want to learn all about finance and marketing and the use of human resources? Isn't this going to unsettle your careful balance of home and work? How will your partner feel if you appear to be shooting up the promotion ladder while he's standing still?

Some women who have no difficulty in justifying a decision to return to work ('after all, I have 30 years ahead of me. They might as well be constructive years') find it surprisingly hard to cope with the prospect of promotion.

TELL ME MORE

It is often much easier to come to a decision if you find out exactly what the new work will entail. Responding by showing interest in this way can give you some 'thinking time' and keeps your options open. Even if you do eventually decline the offer, provided you give well thought-out, sensible reasons, the way is still open for you to be offered other opportunities. If your current family commitments make it impractical for you to take on management responsibilities that entail nights away from home or weekends working, you may well be borne in mind for future opportunities if you make it clear that your family commitments will diminish as your children grow older.

For instance, you might say: 'My son is only just moving from the infant to the junior school. While he's settling down there, I don't want to make any drastic changes to our family routine which works very well. I also feel that if I am going to take on a more responsible job, I want to be able to give it my best efforts – so on this particular occasion I have to say no. I hope there will be other chances in the future.' That's honest and shows you are not just thinking of your family priorities but of the firm's needs, too.

You may have to prompt management to recognize your management potential if, though you're ready for promotion and free to take on the responsibilities involved, they seem to pass you over. One woman wrote to me: 'I even have to type out the notices of vacancies that are posted on our internal noticeboards and it makes me so cross! I could easily have handled the responsibilities of the assistant press officer's job offered recently, but it never occurred to my boss that I might be given first refusal.' If this happens to you, you should first ask yourself whether people realize you want promotion. Someone who does a particular job with efficiency and enthusiasm may be regarded as very content with her circumstances. Moreover, the thought of losing her ability and experience in the area of work concerned may discourage management from offering any alternatives.

If this is your situation, try expressing interest in new jobs as they crop up. If you do happen to be the person who has to type or put up the vacancy details, say 'That sounds an interesting job. I wonder if you'd consider someone with my kind of experience.' You may get any one of a variety of reactions, from the kind-hearted, encouraging 'I don't see why not – have a try' to 'Well, you could apply, but I don't know how I'd manage without you' and 'Oh, no. Though they say "preferably experienced" I'm sure they'll get lots of applicants with appropriate training. Sorry to disappoint you'.

From the reaction you get, you can gauge whether your present manager intends to hang on to you regardless of your own ambitions, or whether you would be helped, or at least not hindered, in seeking promotion.

PROVING POTENTIAL
Apart from expressing interest in advancement, you need to show motivation and knowledge of developments in the area of work concerned. If people know that on your own initiative and in your own time, you're bothering to get knowledge and skills

that could be useful in a more responsible job, then whether you positively apply for promotion or not, they will be aware that you're preparing for advancement. It's one way of drawing yourself to the attention of the people with the power to promote you.

Sometimes it is possible to acquire by evening classes the qualifications that will boost you up the next step of the management ladder. This may have the added advantage of contact with people working in the same speciality, if you are aiming at a qualification in a specific professional area, or of being able to exchange experiences with other potential managers from a range of backgrounds if you decide to take a course in some aspect of business or administration.

If your home responsibilities make evening classes impractical, consider a distance-learning course. The Open University's 'Open Business School' has a range of courses for people with management ambitions, ranging from single-subject courses like 'Accounting and Finance for Managers' and 'Marketing in Action' to a professional Diploma in Management which is one way of entering the MBA programme of the Open Business School. There is also the Access course 'Women Into Management'. It's worth asking if your employer will sponsor you on an OU course: in 1989 more than 80 per cent of Open Business School students were sponsored by their employers.

Individual professional associations can advise you about the availability of distance-learning courses or, sometimes, summer schools you might attend to widen your knowledge. Even if there is no formal course, belonging to a professional association and reading its journal helps you keep abreast of developments in your occupation.

GETTING THE KNOWLEDGE
All too often, professional journals are circulated between executives who give the contents list a quick skim, then pass them on to the next person on the list without paying any attention to anything not directly related to their current interests. More careful study that includes the vacancy columns and information about short courses could be fruitful for anyone who wants to make progress.

If you work in such a specialized field that it does not support a magazine, it may have a newsletter (or you might suggest starting one, when you attend a course or meeting).

As well as taking an interest in the activities of your occupation's professional institute or trade association, you may have the opportunity to join either a women's group connected with your own speciality, eg, Women in Banking, Women in Publishing, City Women's Network, or the local branch of a national organization, such as the UK Federation of Business and Professional Women. Through such groups you can learn more about courses to improve your prospects or employers' efforts to make it easier for women to work, such as career-break schemes.

GETTING YOURSELF KNOWN

As important – perhaps even more important – is the opportunity of developing social contacts within your own field. Some women say it's equivalent in value to the 'old school tie', or less politely the 'public school mafia' enjoyed by some business-people, to belong to a women's campaigning and support group, where you get advance information on opportunities and developments. There's a list of these groups in *Returning to Work* – the book of courses published, appropriately, by the Women Returners' Network.

Whatever your work and wherever your ambitions may lie, it is important to know what's being talked about in your own career area. This is as vital for the woman who is genuinely content with a fairly routine – but essential – job without much promotion potential as for the very ambitious career woman who expects to advance in responsibility at work as her home commitments diminish.

PREPARING FOR CHANGE

We all need to be aware of new techniques being introduced and be ready to adapt our way of working to absorb them, otherwise we limit our scope. This may not seem important to you if you're so happy in your work that you can never envisage wanting to change. Change, though, can be thrust upon you, by anything from a house move to a company takeover.

Changes are often insidious. Among careers writers, I was neither the first nor the last to buy a computer and word-processing system. All the same, when a publisher's contract specified that I should supply 'two copies of the book on disc'

I was surprised, though when mentioning it to friends, some had already become used to handing over a small package of discs instead of a great pile of typewritten manuscript. Recently I took on a new careers column in a family magazine and had to adjust to another development. 'We'd like 117 lines @ 37 characters,' said the commissioning letter. After many years of being asked to write 1,000 or 1,500 words, that was a big change.

Employers who ask for material to be 'faxed' to them rather than posted are now commonplace, and there are moves within journalism, if not publishing, for contributors to be provided with computer modems, systems that link one computer, on the writer's premises, to another computer, in the newspaper or magazine's offices. Once the text is ready, using a special phone connection, it's possible for what appears on the writer's VDU to be seen (and if necessary, edited) on the publication's VDU. This is an example of a development under way in my occupation; there are similar developments in every occupation that can affect your everyday job, and certainly your prospects of advancement if you are not prepared for them.

CAREER BLOCKS

What if you want to progress but find your path is blocked by more senior people in your own company who are the wrong age to be moving on, while your family loyalties make it impossible for you to go further afield to seek advancement? In such a situation, it's worth considering how you can develop and use your particular skills outside work to get satisfaction and enhance your reputation.

I once met a bank manager who was quite surprised to find he'd been singled out to give lectures at the bank's training centre as a result of tutoring students in banking at the local further education college. The connection is obvious enough, but I imagine it was the last thing the manager had in mind when the local FE college first telephoned him to ask if he could help out with some lectures to students of finance.

In my BBC years, interviewees were often people whose views had been quoted in the press, or who had published articles on some subject of general interest in special-interest journals. One or two of these people went on to develop second careers in broadcasting – which in turn did their general career progress no harm! Be responsive when your local radio station asks you to take part in a discussion or phone-in: your Managing Director could be listening.

If you are ambitious but can see no direct route into management from your current employment, then taking responsibility for managing the affairs of a community group, whether it's a youth club or a residents' association, will give you an opportunity to demonstrate your interest in handling people or dealing with accounts or running a fund-raising campaign. Even better, if you take a leading role in the activities of a local branch of your professional institute, you are quite likely to be invited to be the branch representative at national meetings, where your views and experience will be sought. This is a way of attracting the attention of prospective employers as well as influencing your present employer.

Be careful with letters to the press, though; write as an individual, and make it clear that you do so, unless you are specifically invited to put your profession's point of view. As an individual you'll find some sympathizers and some who disagree with your point of view. The latter will still respect you, provided you make it clear that you are not trying to speak on their behalf.

EARNING RECOGNITION
In matters of promotion, as in life generally, you tend to get out what you put in. I am reminded of the secretary of a small professional association who, unpaid, arranged a year's programme of visits and conferences for her fellow members. It involved her in a lot of hard work but inevitably also led to her becoming very well-known by leading employers and training providers in the career concerned. No-one was surprised when she was offered the editorship of a leading journal – and all those who had enjoyed and benefited from her earlier visits and conferences supported her whole-heartedly in her new job.

INVESTING IN YOUR FUTURE
As I write, UK employers and employees look towards the single European market in 1992. The majority, alas, appear to be doing little more than looking: job advertisements rarely ask for knowledge of a language other than English. Colleges, however, are looking ahead, and it's interesting to see the growth of degree courses like Engineering and French or Chemistry and

German. If you liked languages at school, you might give your career prospects a boost by picking up where you left off. Not every job concerned with international marketing involves travelling (which you might regard as impractical if you also have a family for which you are the central figure). People who are able to translate instruction manuals or advertising material into another language have a very valuable skill, as do people who can teach English as a foreign or second language, particularly if they have knowledge of the technical or professional terms used in a particular occupation.

Advancement in a career usually means looking ahead; either getting qualifications that are already highly regarded in your own occupation or in employment generally, or taking a longer-term view and looking for solutions to the kind of problems that get aired at conferences, seminars and in professional journals.

For instance, there has always been a demand for sales training to prepare experts in particular fields to promote the sales of materials, equipment and services to both industry and retailers. But as the use of computers in business grew, some enterprising sales training concerns reacted by setting up specialized training systems for people to be taught how to sell computer systems as their manufacturers competed for business. And when the government's Youth Training Scheme came into being, very little was available in the way of training materials, eg, workbooks, tapes and videos. Now, instead of having to create their own teaching materials, organizers of YTS schemes have a host of specially created teaching materials available.

ROUTES TO PROMOTION

As you can see, it's possible to progress in a career by aiming at a specific kind of management job and making yourself eligible for it by taking appropriate qualifications; by aiming generally at advancement and acquiring skills and qualifications that will be relevant to a range of management jobs; by demonstrating your capabilities through participating in work-related activities via a professional institute or by writing for a professional journal, or possibly undertaking a community activity that develops your management skills – and also by looking ahead for skills likely to be in demand and acquiring them before the majority. This might be described as the 'luck is where preparation meets opportunity' method.

THE CHALLENGE OF EQUALITY

There are few occupations today where being a woman need be a disadvantage. Even in heavy manual industries, increasing use of computers and robotics makes it possible for some jobs to be done as effectively by women as by men. Often in industries once regarded as traditionally male, such as engineering, strenuous efforts are being made to attract women, and to offer them entry concessions and special training schemes from which successful female trainees are snapped up by employers keen to tap a new source of talent.

The very disadvantages faced by women who combine home and career often develop characteristics in them that are fundamental to achievement in any field of employment. The woman who wants to succeed in both a career and a relationship (which could mean caring for an elderly relative or living with a husband/partner and children) must develop organizational ability, initiative, tolerance and staying power. There can be few occupations in which these are not the key qualities for success.

MEMO TO EMPLOYERS

'Good staff', the saying tells us, 'are hard to find', and in this final decade of the twentieth century, they are going to be even harder to find as the number of young people decreases. The most appropriate replacements – women returning to work – will have to be persuaded into employment. For most of them, the return will challenge their ability to cope with the dual responsibility of home and work while updating or retraining for the future.

If you succeed in attracting this sought-after group, remember that keeping them in employment will call for a continuous effort. Mature women who have brought up a family are unlikely to be content for long in jobs without prospects. If your personnel and training policies prove that you give promotion to anyone who shows ability, not only will your returners remain, they will be your best advertisement to other potential employees.

Sources Of Information

Jobcentres

A national network of offices with details of local (and occasionally, national) job vacancies, employment training schemes, the Enterprise Training and Allowance scheme, the Career Development Loans scheme, and other publicly financed sources of employment and training for employment and self-employment.

Careers offices

A service primarily for young people seeking information on careers, higher education and training schemes. Increasingly willing to let adults use their information service. Advice on retraining may be available for returners; always *ask* – if the staff are unable to help you themselves, they may track down an Educational Guidance Centre or give you the name of a Mature Student Adviser at your own further education college.

Employment agencies

These independent agencies find staff for employers who pay them a fee for each person supplied. They do not charge fees for finding jobs (though if an agency provides a service, like preparing your CV, it may charge for this). Agencies place people in permanent and temporary employment and many people who want school holidays off find that 'temping' is a good solution. Most agencies deal mainly with office jobs but some specialize in, say, nursing or sales or engineering staff. The Federation of Recruitment and Employment Services publishes a book listing member agencies and the kind of work each handles (see Appendix 2).

Educational guidance agencies

These are local advisory services, often run on a part-time basis and staffed by advisers on educational opportunities for adults. You may find that your library has the address and opening times of a local EGA; otherwise you can write for a nationwide list (£1) to: The Secretary, Richard Edwards, 58 Pound Lane, Canterbury CT1 2BZ.

Public libraries

These will normally have a section devoted to books and leaflets on careers and education, mostly for reference, though some may be available on loan. They often have prospectuses from local further education colleges; they may also have prospectuses from UK universities, polytechnics and HE colleges. Books listed in Appendix 2 are likely to be available in the public library; if not, the library may be able to borrow them from the central collection for you. Librarians don't just store information, they seek it as well, so if you need to find out the name of a trade journal or national society, ask them for help.

Local colleges	Further Education colleges, Higher Education colleges, Polytechnics and Universities are all likely to have someone on the staff who deals with enquiries from mature students. Check the prospectus (in the public library) first, to see if they name a 'Mature Student Adviser', 'Continuing Education Tutor', 'Adult Education Tutor' or other likely job title. They may advise potential students to write to 'The Registrar' or 'The Principal'. If in doubt, try 'The Information Officer'.
Open University	The OU offers degree and postgraduate courses, single subject 'associate student' courses, continuing education courses, short courses and a range of Open Business School courses, including a Diploma and MBA degree. Send enquiries to: Central Enquiry Service, The Open University, PO Box 71, Milton Keynes MK7 6AG.
Open College	They offer job-related courses, job-hunting courses, small business courses, new skills courses (eg, typing) and updating courses (eg, in electronics). For a prospectus, write to: The Open College, FREEPOST, Manchester M3 8BA.
Open College of the Arts	Courses concentrate on developing creative skills in fields like art and design, photography, writing and sculpture. For a prospectus, write to: Open College of the Arts, FREEPOST, Barnsley, South Yorkshire S70 6BR.

National Institute of Adult Continuing Education	Provides support and information for people who work in adult education and publishes summer and winter editions of *Time to Learn* booklets, detailing residential short courses (week and weekend) in a wide range of subjects (1990 price is £2 each): NIACE, 19b de Montfort Street, Leicester LE1 7GE.
Council for the Accreditation of Correspondence Colleges	Publishes a free list of accredited colleges with details of each one's range of subjects. Please enclose stamped addressed envelope if you write for this list. Write to: CACC, 27 Marylebone Road, London NW1 5JS.
National Extension College	Provides free prospectus of distance-learning courses, many based on 'Flexistudy' learning system whereby students have tutorial links with local colleges for face-to-face tuition. Write to: NEC, 18 Brooklands Avenue, Cambridge CB2 2HN.
Department of Education & Science	Provides information on Teaching as a Career (write to the TASC Unit) and free booklets *Grants to Students* and *Postgraduate Grants*. Write to: DES, Elizabeth House, York Road, London SE1 7PH.
Department of Health	Provides free leaflet on bursaries for paramedical training courses. Write to: Department of Health, North Fylde Central Office, Norcross, Blackpool FY3 3TA.

APPENDIX 2

USEFUL BOOKS

LIST A – BIBLIOGRAPHY

Alston, A. and Miller, R. (1989) *Hours to Suit*, London: Rosters Ltd.

Brady, C. (1987) *The Home Earner*, London: Transworld Publishers.

CBD Research (1988) *Directory of British Associations*, Beckenham: CBD Research Publications.

Careers and Occupational Information Centre (1988) *Occupations 1989*, Bradford: COIC.

(1989) *Working in Self-Employment*, Bradford: COIC.

DES (1989) *Pickup Training Directory* (available in microfiche, computer disc or via Prestel through Training Access Points), Guildford: Guildford Educational Services.

ECCTIS (1989) *Access to Higher Education Directory*, Cheltenham: ECCTIS 2000 Ltd.

(1989) *Educational Credit Transfer*, Cheltenham: ECCTIS 2000 Ltd.

Golzen, G. (1989) *Going Freelance*, London: Kogan Page.

Hawthorne, J. (1989) *30 Ways to Make Money in Writing*, London: Rosters.

Kogan Page (1989) *British Qualifications*, London: Kogan Page.

Korving, M. (1989) *The Kogan Page Mature Student's Handbook 1990*, London: Kogan Page.

(1989) *Running Your Office*, London: BBC Books.

Longman (1989) *Yearbook of Recruitment and Employment Agencies*, Harlow: Longman Group UK Ltd.

Lund Humpheries (1989) *Handbook of Degree and Advanced Courses*, Mansfield: NATFHE & Linneys ESL.
Morrow, J. (1989) *Pre-School Choices*, Harlow: Longman Group UK Ltd.
Onslow, B. (1987) *What Can a Teacher Do Except Teach?*, Bradford: COIC.
Pettit, R. (1981) *Occupation – Self-Employed*, London: Wildwood House Ltd.
Segal, A. (1987) *Careers Encyclopedia*, London: Cassell Educational Ltd.
Stechert, K. (1987) *The Credibility Gap*, Wellington: Thorsons Publishing Group Ltd.
Thurman, J. (1986) *A Doctor – or Else? (4th edition)*, Norwich: Yare Valley Publishers.
Women Returners Network (1989) *Returning to Work*, Harlow: Longman Group UK Ltd.

LIST B – FURTHER READING
Alston, A. and Miller, R. (1987) *Equal Opportunities – A Careers Guide*, London: Penguin Books Ltd.
Ballieu, D. (1988) *Streetwise Franchising*, London: Hutchinson Business Books Limited.
Careers & Occupational Information Centre (1987) *Down to Business*, Bradford: COIC.
Committee of Directors of Polytechnics (1989) *Polytechnics Courses Handbook*, London.
Good, M. and Pages, A. (1989) *Second Chances*, Bradford: COIC.
Hobsons/CRAC (1989) *Directory of Further Education*, Cambridge: Hobsons Publishing PLC.
Korving, M. (1989) *Training For Your Next Career*, London: Rosters Ltd.
Midland Bank (1990) *Checks and Balances*.
Sheed & Ward (1989) *University Entrance 1990 – The Official Guide*, London: Association of Commonwealth Universities.
Summerson, E. and Davies, M. (1986/7) *The Directory of Independent Training & Tutorial Organisations*, Richmond: Trotman.

Syrett, M. and Dunn, C. (1988) *Starting a Business On a Shoestring*, London: Penguin Books Ltd.

Standing Conference of Principals (1989) *Colleges and Institutes of Higher Education*, Ormskirk: Edge Hill College of Higher Education.

INDEX